JumpStart
Your Future

JumpStart
Your Future

A Guide for the College-Bound Christian

Danielle Lee

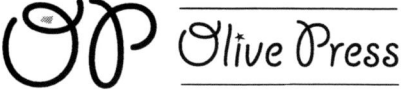

www.jumpstartfuture.com

JumpStart Your Future: A Guide for the College-Bound Christian.

Published by:
The Olive Press
P.O. Box 2056
Stillwater, Minnesota 55082
www.jumpstartfuture.com

Copyright © 2006 by Danielle Lee. All rights reserved. No part of this publication may be produced, stored in a retrieval system, or transmitted in any form or by any means – electronic, mechanical, photocopy, recording, or any other – except for brief quotations in printed reviews, without the prior permission of the publisher.

Scripture taken from the New King James Version. Copyright © 1979, 1980, 1982 by Thomas Nelson, Inc. Used by permission. All rights reserved. PALBEG information was used with permission from Sandi McNamer, the Publications Director of the Wisconsin Department of Public Instruction; P.O. Box 7841; Madison, WI 53707-7841. Phone: (608)266-2188. Toll free, U.S. only: (800)243-8782. Fax: (608)267-9110. "Percentage of Financial Aid Awarded by Type." Reprinted with permission. Minnesota Higher Education Services Office. *Get Ready*. 2004 – 2005 ed. St. Paul, MN: MHESO. P. 22.

Publisher's Cataloging-in-Publication
Quality Books, Inc.

Lee, Danielle
JumpStart your future : a guide for the college-bound Christian/ Danielle Lee.
   p. cm.
Includes biographical references and index.
ISBN-13: 9780976929895
ISBN-10: 0976929899
A college preparation guide for teenage Christians that offers guidance in exploring careers and colleges, applying for financial aid, developing the research and study-skills needed for college-level courses, and approaching campus life and the classroom from a Christian perspective. Ages 15-18.

   1. College student orientation – United States – Juvenile literature. 2. Christian college students – United States – Religious life – Juvenile literature. 3. College choice – United States – Juvenile literature. 4. Universities and colleges – United States – Admission – Juvenile literature. [1. College student orientation. 2. Christian college students. 3. College choice. 4. Universities and colleges.]

I. Title. II. Title: JumpStart your Future.
LB2343.32.L44 2006   378.1`98`0973
QB106-600018   LCCN 2006900150

Proofreading by Sandy Zilka
Cover and Book Layout Design by Tonya Johnson, Freelance Designer
Printed in the United States of America

*For our boys,
Caleb and Ethan,
that they would
live boldly
with love
for Christ.*

Acknowledgments

I am so grateful for all the people and resources that the Lord
placed in my life to make this book possible.
First, I want to thank Josh, my true friend,
for his love, support, and honest feedback.

I'm also thankful for my parents,
for their integrity and wisdom.

A huge thanks goes out to Tonya
for a beautiful book layout and cover design.

Of the many teachers in my life,
I truly appreciate the passion, dedication, and examples of
Pastor Lloyd Johnson, Dr. Scheurman, Mr. Halsey,
Miss Kampen, and Mrs. Bluhm.

I also want to thank my students,
for their humor and teachable spirits.
They are the inspiration behind this book.

To the many authors God has used
to make a difference in my life, I'm thankful for
Lee Strobel, R.C. Sproul, John Piper, Leland Ryken, James W. Sire,
Gladys Hunt, Barbara Hughes, and Jean Fleming.

Most importantly, I want to thank Jesus Christ, my personal Savior,
for giving me the desire to serve and honor Him in all things.
He has irreversibly changed the course of my life.
To Him be the glory.

Foreword

For many students and their parents, going to college has become a haphazard adventure. It's the next thing to do—a rite of passage, rather than a thoughtful decision. This book contains a gold mine of information about what it means to be a college student. Resources for making decisions, information about scholarships and work study programs, helpful hints on how to study and do research, what it means to think critically about ideas–and more–are included in this book. I am amazed at how many parents and youth leaders send graduates off to the university without helping them build a Christian world/life view, or even knowing what it means to think "Christianly." The potential of this book to give students a headstart in maturity and clear thinking is cause for anyone working with young people to thank Danielle Lee for her thorough presentation.

Gladys M. Hunt
Author of *Honey for a Teen's Heart*

JumpStart Your Future
A Guide for the College-Bound Christian

TABLE OF CONTENTS

Acknowledgments

Introduction – Journey

Part 1 – Plan

Chapter 1: Unlock the Mystery – Exploring Career Options 1
- A Crossroad
- Hints for the Hunt
- Options to Explore
- What's Happening Now

Chapter 2: Open the Doors to Your College Search 9
- Finding the Differences
- Comparison-Shopping for Education?
- Take the Campus Tour
- The College Admissions Essay
- One Student's Response

Chapter 3: Hidden Opportunities of Financial Aid 19
- Scholarships: Applications and Essays
- Grants
- Work-Study
- Reciprocity
- Government Service Programs
- Tax Benefits
- Loans

Part 2 – Prepare

Chapter 4: Don't Just Survive, Thrive! 28
- Focus on Priorities
- Plan Ahead
- Take Good Notes
- How Do You Learn Best?
- Gather Your Materials
- Down to Business/Memory Techniques
- Taking the Test

Chapter 5: Communicate in the Classroom 41
- Getting the Most from Your Textbook
- Reading for Discussion

TABLE OF CONTENTS CONTINUED

Chapter 6: Rave Reviews on the Research Paper 46
    Meaningful Research
    Plan Your Approach
    Study the Skeleton
    Strategies for Smooth Research
    Personal Research Checklist

Chapter 7: Warnings from a Whale: Your Guide to the Internet . . . 59
    Advantages and Disadvantages of Internet Research
    Watch Out!
    Determine the Reliability of a Source
    Explore Your Resources
    Search Engine Strategies

Chapter 8: Character at College 67
    A Christian Student's Calling
    Traits of a Good Student

Part 3 – Purpose

Chapter 9: Worlds Apart 75
    Defining a Worldview
    Why Bother?
    A World of Differences
    Finding Absolutes
    A Worldview Exposed

Chapter 10: Break the Mold 84
    The Christian Mind
    What it Means to Think Critically
    Qualities of Critical Thinking

Chapter 11: Between the Lines 92
    Life in the Real World
    Thinking Between the Lines
    Supporting Your Beliefs
    A Case Study

Chapter 12: Preparation for Life 100
    Success in the Details
    Making It Personal

Recommended Reading. 105

Endnotes. 113

Index 119

As for me, I will see your face in righteousness;
I shall be satisfied when I awake in your likeness.

— Psalm 17:15

Journey

It was mid-September in Minnesota – perfect timing to catch the fall colors from Lookout Ridge. My fiancé, Josh, and I filled a backpack with a few snacks, then we headed out along the Superior Hiking Trail. The main trail is a 205-mile stretch, just north of Duluth up to Canada, but we decided to take one of its offshoots. We'd heard that this one would give us a spectacular view of Lake Superior.

The crisp fall air smelled sweet. At first, the path was easy with a few rocks and scrubby pines scattered on either side, but as we hiked, the trees grew denser. At times, we had to jump over unexpected streams. We even crossed a few rough spots where rocks sent the water cascading down in miniature waterfalls. The trees grew even thicker, and soon underbrush branched out along the trail. However, sunlight still shot through small openings in the pines.

The higher we climbed, the harder it was to distinguish the trail. At times, we wondered if we were even on the path. If it weren't for the occasional signs marking the trail, we would have been confused. Sometimes we'd have to backtrack, realizing we'd veered into the woods. By the time we reached Lookout Ridge, we were exhausted and out of breath. But the view from the top made it worth the effort. It was amazing!

"It looks like an ocean," I said, as we gazed out over the water on our right. From this spot, we could just barely see the ridge of Wisconsin on the horizon. To our left, blazing red and fiery orange maples were speckled with dots of yellow and brown from the birch trees. Throughout the scene, dark green pines grew in clusters.

Our journey in life often imitates a winding trail. Sometimes it's easy, but sometimes it's really hard. Sometimes the path is clear, but sometimes we feel lost. There are even occasions when we have to circle back to study and rethink the directions from the last signpost.

It's hard at times to know which direction to take. Questions spring up. What is God's will for my life? Where should I start if I don't know what God has planned for me? Which college should I choose? How will I pay for college once I am there? Will I do well in my classes? How should I prepare?

When I feel that I've reached a dead end or I have to go back and relearn something, it's easy to get discouraged. In spite of uncertainty and doubts, God guides and directs. In my own life, I've dealt with the same issues you face as a college-bound student. Sometimes it's hard to know God's design, but I'm encouraged by an omniscient God who knows my future. Jeremiah 29:11 says, "For I know the thoughts that I think for you, says the Lord, thoughts of peace and not evil, to give you a future and a hope." Although this promise was given to the Israelites who were exiled in Babylon at the time, I can still claim this principle as a Christian. God has a plan for my future.

So what qualifies me to write on this subject? Quite simply, I've been there. During high school, I fought an internal battle over the college and career search – especially when my best friend was moving for Los Angeles, some 1,500 miles away. As a college student, I also struggled with how to be a witness for Christ in the college classroom. Now that I'm a teacher, I work with college-bound students. My desire is to equip them with the tools necessary to make sound decisions in the years ahead, and that is also my desire for you.

My hope is simply to serve as a signpost at this time in your life. However, there are many other great books and references out there. I will highlight some of the best in Recommended Reading, listed at the end of this book. I hope that you will use some of these as you continue your journey to college.

A CLEAR DIRECTION

The stories in each chapter are based on real situations. They came either from my own experiences or from stories told to me by friends, students, teachers, and professors. Before we begin, however, I feel it's important for you to know where I'm coming from.

My desire is to assist you in becoming a godly man or woman who is able to reason and think because of a strong foundation on God's Word. The Bible provides clear solutions to all of life's problems. In a culture packed with a wide range of worldviews, there is growing apathy toward absolute truth – the truth that it is only through Jesus Christ and His work that we are made righteous before our Creator. This knowledge of a very real and living God makes life worth living.

Right now, you're at a crossroad in life. The decisions you make at this point and in the next few years will influence your future. I'm not really talking about the big decisions, although these are important; it's the details of your life that matter. It's who you are as a person and your relationship to Christ that counts in the end.

Mom and Dad cannot hold your hand forever. As you embark on this journey, I hope that you will remain firm in your convictions as a strong witness for Christ. Your personal relationship with Him is much more important than your school of choice, your dream job, or even the person you'll marry.

Of course, this book may challenge your perception of education. Real life does not pause when you step foot on campus and resume when you leave. College isn't just a place to earn a degree and have some fun for four (or more) years. Even though it can be fun, that's not the ultimate goal. However, earning a 4.0 is not the ultimate goal, either. College is simply a preparation for life ahead. It's part of the process of becoming the person God has designed you to be. With that purpose in mind, we can begin our plans for the future.

Part 1 – Plan

> Everyone has his own specific vocation or mission in life to carry out a concrete assignment which demands fulfillment. Therein he cannot be replaced, nor can his life be repeated. Thus, everyone's task is as unique as his specific opportunity to implement it.[1]

CHAPTER 1

Unlock the Mystery
Exploring Career Options

"Traffic along Interstate 94 appears to be at a standstill –"

No kidding, I thought as I clicked off the radio. To avoid overheating the engine, I turned off my air conditioning, but the sun's heat continued to beat down on my car. I stared ahead. The bumper sticker in front of me hadn't changed. Boldly, it announced, "He who dies with the most toys wins." After watching it blankly for a while, I started to think about what it actually meant.

Success. Webster calls it "the achievement of something planned or attempted." Of course, that 'something' depends a lot on a person's goals and desires. By that bumper sticker's standard, success is measured in *stuff*. But a lot of people measure success with other yardsticks, like intelligence or popularity. A Christian's view of success, though, is different, or at least it should be.

Take a moment to write down – or simply consider – your goals. A year from now, will you be successful? What about five or ten years from now? Use your imagination.

At the beginning of a job search, my students ask many questions. *Which college should I go to? What classes should I take? What if I don't know which career to pursue?* They're trying to figure out God's plan for their lives. To be honest, I don't know all those answers, and I tell them that. But I do know this: God has a plan, and He will be faithful to reveal that plan in His time as we relax and learn to trust Him.

"That doesn't help me know what job to choose," one student said in frustration.

But he was missing the point. If we are to succeed in life – regardless of the job or present circumstances – all that we are to be about is bringing glory to God through every thought, decision, and act (Ecclesiastes 12:13). This is true success according to God's standards.

The details reveal one's degree of success in life. There is much to do if we only look around and take advantage of these God-given opportunities. We can't just wait around for something to happen. Instead, we have to get busy in what God has given us *right now*. In doing so, we will find purpose as we seek to honor Christ in the little things. This is especially true when Christians use their gifts and abilities to serve others.

For a Christian, this isn't just going through the motions – of being religious or even moral. True success is glorifying Christ *with joy*. Specifically, it's being teachable in our mistakes; it's fully enjoying all that God has created; and it's serving others so that they may experience a little of Christ's work in our lives. In a highly recommended book, *Don't Waste Your Life*, John Piper writes,

> *We waste our lives when we do not pray and think and dream and plan and work toward magnifying God in all spheres of life. God created us for this: to live our lives in a way that makes him look more like the greatness and beauty and the infinite worth that he really is.*[2]

Success really is in the details.

A CROSSROAD

With tough decisions to make, you've come to a fork in the road. If you haven't experienced it yet, you'll hear the question, "So, what do you want to do with your life?" This question gets old, especially if you don't have answers. You may even find yourself asking, *What is God's will for my life?*

While you may not have answers to all the details, there is hope. We don't have to worry. Instead, in I Peter 5:7, we're to cast all our cares away because He cares for us. God, in His wisdom, guides and directs. In fact, we're even commanded *not* to worry about the future in Matthew 6:34: "Therefore, do not worry about tomorrow, for tomorrow will worry about its own things. Sufficient for the day is its own trouble."

As we rely on the Lord to guide us, we still have a responsibility to prepare for the future. Proverbs is full of pictures of preparation and hard work. As Proverbs 16:9 says, "A man's heart plans his way, but the Lord directs his steps." In relation to the career search, it's all about balance – the combination of effort on our end with complete reliance on God for direction. Problems and uncertainty become clear when we simply do what is right before Him.

Pray for Direction – In spite of the unknown, we can rely on the Lord for direction and appreciate what He has already given us. So pray. How would God have you serve Him? Sincerely ask the Lord to guide you in what He has planned for your life – not the ideals you've always envisioned or the expectations and pressures formed by someone else for your life. As Proverbs 16:3 says, "Commit your works to the Lord, and your thoughts will be established."

Trust God's Plan – As you pray, trust that the Lord will show you what to do. Although most people like clear directions, we can't always see what God has planned. He ultimately controls our lives and allows events and situations to bring about His purpose. Romans 8:28, says "And we know that all things work together for good to those who love God, to those who are the called according to His purpose."

Follow His Lead – True peace comes when we relax and patiently trust God. "Trust in the Lord, and do good; dwell in the land, and feed on his faithfulness. Delight yourself also in the Lord, and He shall give you the desires of your heart. Commit your way to the Lord, trust also in Him, and He shall bring it to pass" (Psalm 37:3 – 5). I love these verses because they show a clear picture of a quiet and calm heart that's fixed on the Lord.

Carry On – Every step in the process must be done to the best of our abilities. That calls for excellence in the little things. "And whatever you do, do it heartily, as to the Lord and not to men, knowing that from the Lord you will receive the reward of the inheritance; for you serve the Lord Christ" (Colossians 3:23 – 24).

God has designed a plan for our lives. As we learn to pray and trust Him, a deeply satisfying peace results. This knowledge enables us to go ahead with plans until the Lord shuts the door. "The burning question for most Christians should be: How can my life count for the glory of God in my job?"[3] Piper answers this question by explaining that, *no matter the career*, we bring God glory by our continual fellowship with Him throughout the day. We honor Him with our creativity and industry, by confirming and enhancing the truths of the Bible, by using our resources, such as money, to help others, and by viewing our web of relationships as a gift to share the Gospel and live out what we claim to believe.[4]

HINTS FOR THE HUNT

There are many resources available to help you discover God's direction for your future. Some of these books are discussed in the section at the end of this book called Recommended Reading. For now, the following suggestions offer a road map to get you started in your career search.

1) Reflect. As you consider areas of interest, think back on the talents and skills God has given you. Quite often, people find it helpful to write in a journal to help sort through ideas on paper. Take time to reflect and respond to the following questions from Michael Landes' book, *The Backdoor Guide to Short-Term Job Adventures*. As you write, you might begin noticing patterns and areas that appeal to you.

- What kind of person do you want to be?
- To what (and whom) do you gravitate toward naturally?
- What are your values?
- What are your unique qualities?

- What are your passions?
- What are five skills you enjoy using?
- What three words best describe you?
- What are your dreams and fears?
- Where do you need improvement?
- What do your friends say you are good at?
- Whom do you admire?
- What traits of those you admire would you make your own?
- Putting money aside, what job would give you the most satisfaction?
- If you could begin any hobby, what would that be?[5]

2) Brainstorm. Create a list of intriguing job options. For help with ideas, refer again to that list of Recommended Reading. Begin to research your options by finding out about the career. Jot down basic information: What is the job description? What education or experience do you need? Gradually whittle down the list until you get a few that really interest you.

3) Explore. Investigate your top job choices more deeply, and be realistic. Try to find out as much about the actual working experience as possible. For example, I knew a student named Eric who wanted to become a teacher – until he realized how much preparation was involved. The average teacher prepares lessons (which involves research), modifies those lessons for students with learning disabilities, grades projects and papers, returns phone calls from parents and students, attends teachers' meetings or conferences, and maintains a teacher's license. He also learned how much teachers are actually paid. On the flip side, he thought about how amazing it would be to watch students learn and grow over time. He also appreciated the flexibility and creativity in designing lesson plans. In addition, he knew that he'd have all holidays and summers off. Like Eric, you'll need to explore the pros and cons behind your own career choice as you investigate the daily realities of the job. Could this job really work for you?

4) Interview. Find knowledgeable professionals in the field who are truly passionate about what they do. Ask if they would be willing to meet with you as you may be considering a career in this field. The following questions from the great resource, *Cool Careers for Dummies*, should get you started, although you may be able to think of more that relate to your specific field.

- How did you get into this career?
- Can you walk me through a typical day?
- What do you find to be the best and worst parts about your job?

- What have you found to be the skills most important to succeeding in your career?
- Can you think of anything you know now that you wish you had known when you were deciding to enter this field?
- Can you think of anything I should know about this field that is unlikely to find its way into print?
- Describe your background and interests. Then ask, 'Do you think I should consider this field? Are there any other fields I should consider?'
- Do you have any advice about the smartest way to prepare for this career?
- Are there jobs in this field that provide particularly good learning experiences?
- In this field, where are good job openings listed?
- What kind of salary can I expect?
- Are there any particularly interesting specialties within your field?
- How is the field changing?
- Why might someone leave this field?
- Do you know of anything I should read before deciding whether to pursue this career? Any event I should attend? Any organization I should join?
- Is there any other advice you would give someone entering this field?[6]

5) Job Shadow. Experience a job firsthand. At this point in your search, there is hardly a better way to learn about a career. In fact, this experience could save you a lot of time, money, and effort if you discover, for example, that being a veterinarian is not exactly what you had imagined. Watching someone do the work you're about to train for could save you weeks or even years of schooling. On the other hand, job shadowing may actually confirm your interest in the field. If you know someone in your desired field – an acquaintance, friend of the family, relative, or member of your church – ask if you can follow him for a day. (You may need to look up a number in the Yellow Pages if you don't know anyone in this field.) In some situations, you may even get to participate. The point is that if you really want to work in this field, you should try it for at least one day. Sometimes, expectations are quite different from reality. You don't want to finish college only to find that the field you chose is boring, unchallenging, or draining.

6) Volunteer. While you're still in high school, consider getting involved in a volunteer opportunity. For example, you might work at the Salvation Army, spend time with seniors, or offer a hand at the place where you job-shadowed. Do you feel God might be calling you to the mission field? Try a short-term missions trip. One young man I know, Dan, had no idea what field to enter upon graduation. Frustrated, he decided not to enter college because he felt he would be wasting money without a direction. Dan found a job in carpentry and remodeling with his two older brothers, but he still felt restless. After a couple of years, there was still no joy or satisfaction at the end of each day. Finally, Dan heard about a short-term missions opportunity in Australia. After praying about it, he decided to go. Within a few months, he became a full-time staff member within the mission's organization. Now, Dan's excitement bubbles over because he has peace with where God has placed him. Of course, this does not imply that everyone must be in a foreign country to be serving the Lord. We can and should serve Him with joy – regardless of our location.

7) Study Abroad. Even as a high school student, you can take part of a summer to study abroad. One such opportunity is People-to-People International at <http://www.ptpi.org>. Founded by President Eisenhower in 1956, this program sends student ambassadors to other countries to experience and gain an appreciation for other cultures.

Any of these approaches may open your eyes to new options in your career search. Whether you try one or two tips or attack all seven, it's important to seek the Lord first and talk about your options with your parents. Then you can reflect on your abilities, research options, carry out interviews, and explore other avenues, like job-shadowing, volunteering, or studying abroad. During this process, pay attention and use each opportunity to think realistically about how your options would be as a job.

CAREER EXPLORATIONS

Whether you will continue your education after high school depends largely on the career you choose. To help you investigate your job choice and its daily realities, you can explore this career through writing. At this point, focus on one career from the list you created earlier.

Once you have honed in on a career that truly interests you, investigate anything you can find on that topic. Visit your favorite bookstore and search the section on careers. Check material out at the library. Surf the web. Talk to professionals in the field. Line up interviews. Make an appointment to job shadow. All this effort is exciting because it's about your future. What you are doing at this point is gathering information, because you'll want to include the following in your paper:

- Job Description: What are the unique responsibilities or special requirements of this job? Will you deal primarily with people, information and words, or objects?
- Educational or Experiential Requirements: What education or job training

do you need to take to prepare for this job? How much will this cost you in time and money?
- Primary Source: Can you find an eyewitness, a professional in the field, to interview about this career?
- Job Shadowing: Are you able to follow this person for a day in his field?
- Reality Check: What are the pros and cons of this career?
- Job Outlook: What is the need for this career choice in the real world?
- Salary and Benefits: What is the starting wage or salary and any benefits to the job?
- Is there any other relevant information that adds to your overall impression?

Refer to Chapters 7 and 8 later in this book to guide you through the writing process. The written portion of this project should include the elements of a solid research paper and follow the strategies of research. You'll also discover information on the Modern Language Association (MLA) standards for quoting and citing sources within your paper.

In gathering your information for this project, do your homework. Preparation is key before you choose your primary source to interview. Find a minimum of four different types of sources to get the most accurate representation of the career. For example, use an interview as your primary source and find at least one book, one magazine, and one internet article. This will help you avoid a smattering of random internet articles.

In my own classes, students present their material in the first person, pretending that they really do work in that field. Quite often, students also dress in costume or bring career props for extra credit. For example, an "engineer" came to class with a long-sleeved collared shirt, a few pens, his notebook, and a calculator, while the "carpenter" came to class with a hard hat and a tool belt filled with a hammer and nails, a straight-edge ruler, a carpenter's pencil, and a tape measure. These costumes set the scene for students to speak in character. Although you may not be in a classroom setting, I would suggest at least presenting your findings to your family or other "audience."

SEEING GOD'S PLAN

As you pursue God's direction for your life, think about how God might be using you to influence others. As J.P. Moreland writes in his book, *Love Your God with All Your Mind*, a Christian goes to college to discover his career, but he should also go to become an influence for Christ in our culture.[7] Of course, this reality is not so much in *what* we do as *how* we do it. As Ecclesiastes 9:10 says, "Whatever your hand finds to do, do it with your might..."

You might still be unsure about your career, but what are you doing right now? No matter the task or the job, we are sent forth by God,

> *To work as his image-bearers; our ditches are to be dug straight, our pipe-fittings are not to leak, our cabinet corners should be flush, our surgical incisions should be clean, our word processing accurate and appealing, and our meals nutritious and attractive, because God is a God of order and beauty and competence... the essence of our work as humans must be that it is done in conscious reliance on God's power, and in conscious quest of God's pattern of excellence, and in deliberate aim to reflect God's glory.*[8]

Are you a son or daughter? Are you a student? Are you an employee? No matter our role or position *at the moment*, we have a high calling to honor God in the details. The point here is to be open for a change of direction – regardless of whether or not you *think* you know what God wants for your future.

Accept change. Try something new. Be realistic with the time, energy, and money you have to get you where you would like to go.

Open the Doors to
Your College Search

CHAPTER 2

In a darkened theater, spotlights swirl through the crowd. Suddenly, the announcer's voice booms out your name. "Congratulations! You are the next contestant on..." But you haven't heard anything else. Your heart pounds wildly as you leap from the chair, fumbling over knees and shoes to get to the center aisle. The crowd erupts in applause while you race toward the stage. The next few minutes are a blur, but you suddenly find yourself facing a major decision. You are informed that you have precisely ten seconds to choose either Curtain Number One or Curtain Number Two before the sound of the buzzer. That simple choice will determine your immediate future. Your mind quickly recalls the possibilities: an all-expenses-paid, round-trip for four to the Bahamas – or an empty stage, sending you home empty.

Toward the end of high school, you may be feeling a similar tension about college. This "curtain choice" for college calls out through billboards, commercials, and even spam. Letters bombard your mailbox from community colleges, private schools, and your state university. So which "curtain" should you choose?

Fortunately, this choice is a little different from the ten-second decision on a game show. In Proverbs 16:9, we read, "A man's heart plans his way, but the Lord directs his steps." This knowledge brings an incredible sense of peace when we trust Him.

While trust brings security, fear creates all kinds of problems. We don't have to hope that we're making the right decision, though. We can be confident that the Lord will show us His direction in life – even if it's not the answer we expect. In James 1:5-6, we learn how to pray about such life-impacting decisions, like choosing a college:

If any of you lacks wisdom, let him ask of God, who gives to all liberally and without reproach and it will be given him. But let him ask in faith, with no doubting, for he who doubts is like a wave of the sea driven and tossed by the wind. As you seek the Lord's direction, your path will begin to unfold. You can then proceed with confidence as you research your options.

Although it's a thrill to make you own decisions, consider the advice from Proverbs 11:14: "Where there is no counsel, the people fall; but in the multitude of counselors, there is safety." Proverbs 15:22 adds, "Without counsel, plans go awry, but in the multitude of counselors, they are established." Today, the perception of asking parents for advice is not cool. It's hard to imagine that they really faced the same situations and could provide useful insight. However, these verses show us that with advice, plans take shape, bringing confidence in decisions. The bigger the decision, the more important it should be to seek advice. Even presidents have a trusted group of advisors, like Andrew Jackson, whose advisors quietly met behind the scenes in the kitchen of the White House.

FINDING THE DIFFERENCES

While seeking advice, gather as much as you can about your choices. Research the facts and try to be objective as you answer the following questions. Your responses can help you recognize which type of school meets your unique situation.

- Why do you want to go to college?
- What is special about this school? Does it offer a specialized program?
- What are your goals? What do you expect to learn and prepare for as you begin this course?
- Will the size of the campus make a difference to you?
- What is the classroom setting like? Will you be able to interact with the professors?
- How will you pay for college?

As you consider these questions, it's important to understand how schools differ. These features help you identify what each school offers as you determine which meets your needs the best. In the chart below, study the differences between a typical community college, a private college, or your state university. Which factors influence your decision the most? If it helps, circle the items that appeal to you.

Category	Community College	Private College	State University
History	Relatively new. Established within the last 100 years.	The oldest form of American higher education. (Harvard began in 1636.)	Publicly or privately funded institutions; often established in the 1800s.
Purpose	"Stepping stone" offers general courses which transfer elsewhere for completion of four-year degree; also offers short-term training or specialization in vo-tech programs.	Offers a broad education in arts, sciences, and humanities and is often affiliated with a religious denomination.	Offers a range of degrees and often has grants set aside for conducting research.
Size of Campus	Small – in the sense that it serve the local community.	Varies – from less than 1,000 to sometimes more than 10,000.	Large – enrollment can be in the upper thousands.
Cost of Tuition	Less expensive, and because of location, students may pace themselves on the number of classes taken.	Often expensive because it is generally privately funded. However, look for financial aid packages.	Varies from state to state. For out-of-state residents, check for reciprocity eligibility.
Classroom Experience	Develops the learning experience for either hands-on job training or continuing education elsewhere.	Focus is on academics. More personal because of individual attention; students may be known by name. Competitive.	Because of classroom size, may have large classes, which tend to be less personal.
Body Life	A range of ages from high school students in the Post-Secondary Education Option (PSEO) to older, returning students.	More opportunities for involvement.	Diverse. Offers a wide range of extracurricular activities. Students from a variety of backgrounds.
Housing	Because of its location, many commute from home or apartment. Some on-campus housing is available.	Residential halls are available and sometimes even required for the first year or two.	Dormitories and fraternity/sorority housing available, as well as off-campus housing.

From this chart, you should be able to recognize the major differences between schools. Compare the advantages and disadvantages one type of school might have over another. If you circled the most appealing features, you may already be able to narrow down some of your options.

COMPARISON-SHOPPING FOR EDUCATION?

You may have taken Home Economics in high school. In a class like that, you most likely learned about comparison-shopping – you know, that project where you had to check different cans of soup for their price per ounce. Well, magnify that comparison-shopping on a grand scale, and you have the college search.

Simply stated, comparison-shopping for a college is the next step in helping you identify the details surrounding your college choice. However, keep in mind that few things will influence this choice as much as a personal tour of the campus. Because a personal tour is not always possible at this point in the process, most schools provide a website geared toward answering your basic questions about their campus. Many even offer virtual tours and perceptions of the school from real students. These students may share their reasons for choosing the school, special features about campus life, and other enrichment opportunities. Keep in mind, though, that these students have been carefully selected to put the school in the best light. If you're looking for a more natural response, I'll offer some ideas to get the most from your campus tour shortly. However, the following questions can serve as a possible guide in beginning your research:

- Will distance influence your choice? How will a long-distance school affect me, as opposed to attending a local school? (For example, consider the cost of airfare, car payments and/or insurance, parking fees, gas, maintenance, bus fare, etc.) Would you consider any other alternatives, such as online courses, for long-distance schools?

- How does the cost of tuition compare between community colleges, private schools, state universities, and special interest schools? Would transferring from a community college to a private school be a good option?

- What is the difference between the cost of tuition alone and the cost when room and board are added? What other factors should you consider when making the decision to live either on or off campus, at home, or in an apartment? Possible responses may include convenience, transportation, extra-curricular involvement, outside employment versus the work-study option on campus, more independence and social interaction with the student body, and levels of self-motivation, responsibility, and ability to ignore distractions.

- What financial aid opportunities are available, such as scholarships, grants, reciprocity, or work study programs?

- What is the size of the campus? How does the campus size compare or contrast to my experience? What concerns or expectations do I have regarding the size of the campus?

- How does the student-to-instructor ratio differ from one school to the next? How difficult will it be for me to interact with instructors?

- What is the percentage of graduates who find jobs in their fields after they earn their degree? Is there a list of employers who have hired graduates in this field?

- What facilities and/or equipment does this school offer related to my field? (For example, a school that specializes in theater and the performing arts may offer little to the student interested in computer technology because the institute's budget simply can't afford the latest lab equipment and training.) If there is equipment, is it up-to-date and in a solid working condition?

○ What extracurricular activities does the institute offer? How easy would it be for me to participate? (Some schools offer full-ride scholarships for athletes who excel in certain sports, making them highly competitive.)

These questions are just meant to spark thought and discussion. If you are a visual learner, you might want to log your findings on a chart similar to the one below.

College Comparison-Shopping Chart

Category	School A	School B	School C	School D
Type of college				
Religious affiliation				
Location (distance from home)				
Cost of tuition				
Room and board				
Financial aid opportunities				
Size of campus				
Student to teacher ratio				
% of job placement after graduation				
Facilities and/or equipment				
Extracurricular opportunities				
Miscellaneous				

Take the time to chart your answers. The information will help you look at your college options objectively, which will simplify the college decision and give you real facts to talk over with your parents or mentors. Once you have shared your results with others, you'll be better able to whittle down your list of school choices.

TAKE A TOUR

The next step in the college search is to set aside a day (or take a short trip with your parents) to check out your top college choices. The best time for such a trip is during the fall of your senior year. If you're already beyond that point, just be sure to visit when regular classes are in session. However, don't go during vacation or homecoming. The two extremes – an empty campus or a school buzzing with excitement – will not give you an accurate feel for the realities of daily life. Be alert. You want to squeeze the most out of this visit as you make your decision.

Before visiting, jot down a list of questions to ask or details you want to find out in person. You don't have to carry a notebook like an investigator while you tour, but at least stick the paper in your pocket as a reminder!

While you visit, you'll want to explore the whole campus: buildings, classrooms, the library, help centers, dorm rooms, the cafeteria, and any other special features on campus. Don't be shy in approaching students. Casually ask why they chose this school. Are they happy with their program? How do they feel about the professors?

Don't just limit yourself to asking students, though. Chances are, you'll find a professor in your field who is available during your visit. He may be able to answer any questions you still have and give information about his background at the school and current projects. What you're doing here is finding out how he *still* feels about his field.

Immediately after the tour, make a note of your reactions, especially if you're visiting more than one campus. In what ways has your opinion changed now that you've seen the campus? What highlights stand out? What areas concern you? Discussing your reactions with your parents or guidance counselor can give you even more insight.

THE COLLEGE ADMISSIONS ESSAY

All right. You've narrowed down your favorite college choices. Now you just have to apply. However, writing the college admissions essay can be intimidating because acceptance is partly based on this response.

Don't be alarmed, though. The important point to remember is to be natural. Remember that there is a two-fold purpose in writing the college admissions essay. First, the college admissions board simply wants to know about you, the prospective student. They will consider several factors, such as the experiences that have shaped you into who you are today, your personal character traits, and the qualities you'll bring to the campus.

The second purpose of writing the college admissions essay is to make connections between your experiences and personal growth. Frank Leana, in his article, "Application Essays: Finding a Personal Voice," gives this advice:

> *Before we can be clear about what our experiences have meant to us and begin to state what we want next, we need to evaluate those experiences, weigh our wins against our losses and do some critical self-assessment.*[9]

Writing the college admissions essay should be viewed as an exciting opportunity to see what changes have shaped your life. Typically, your school will ask you to respond to at least one of the following topics in 500 words or less:

- Discuss a significant experience or achievement in your life.
- Discuss an issue of personal, local, or national concern and its importance to you.
- If you could interview any person in the arts, politics, religion, or science, whom would you choose and why?
- How would your best friend describe your strengths and weaknesses?
- Who has been the most influential person in your life? In what ways was he or she influential?

The dilemma that many students face is what to write about. While some students may choose to write about a pivotal moment in their lives, *these responses do not have to be about a tragic or monumental experience*. For example, one question asks the student to evaluate a significant experience or achievement that has special meaning in his or her life. Students may choose to write about how a job gave them more confidence and social skills in business or how their role in 4-H developed leadership skills. These topics help you to evaluate an experience and communicate personal growth.

Perhaps the most practical and straightforward advice concerning this essay comes from a book packed with real responses, *Best College Admissions Essays*.

> *Don't try to sell yourself or prove how great you are, how smart you are, or how accomplished you are. Your definitive theories and brilliant solutions to global problems will not impress the reader. Admit it: You have more questions than answers at this point in your life. Use your essay as an opportunity to wonder about life, to pose thoughtful questions, and to probe and investigate, not to tell the reader the way it is.*[10]

Although this advice is blunt, it highlights an important point: Be real.

In addition, consider the following advice from *100 Successful College Application Essays*:

- Write your essay, *not* for some imaginary admissions officer, but for yourselves.
- Consider simply telling a story because it's most natural.
- Invest some time in reading some good writing before sitting down to write your own essay.
- Be sure your essay reflects you, and not some idealized version of yourself that you have come to imagine.

- Don't ask the essay to carry too heavy a load with name-dropping of alumni or rationalizing low grades.
- Sort and sift any advice you receive and settle on that which intuitively makes sense to you.[11]

As with any writing assignment you've had in high school, you need an opening hook – something to grab your readers and keep them interested. Ideas include a great quote, a thoughtful question, an observation, a definition, a personal experience, or a confession.

When ending your essay, bring closure. End any suspense and answer any questions you have posed earlier. Whatever you do, be creative. Don't address the admissions committee and beg them to admit you. Don't use boring words like "finally" or "in conclusion." And don't end your essay with a question.[12]

Before you send out the essay, critique what you have written. Are your thoughts organized, unified, and focused? Is your response in-depth, showing creativity, originality, and sincerity? Have you checked spelling, punctuation, sentence structure, and word usage? Once you've revised your writing to the best of your abilities, ask someone to read your essay and give you an honest first impression.

ONE STUDENT'S RESPONSE

The following essay is a sample student response to the question: "If one of your closest friends were to be interviewed about your greatest strengths and weaknesses, how would he respond?"

Imagine a reporter interviewing your best friend. Your friend is asked to describe your strengths and weaknesses. As I imagine this scene in my own life, here is what I hope my friend would say:

"To explain Lisa's strengths and weaknesses, I'd have to give you a preface. She grew up learning Biblical values. Her parents had strong moral values and instilled them in their children. From her family's beliefs, she learned early in life the benefit of things like sharing, honesty, obedience, and kindness.

"Lisa has always loved anything which requires imagination. Growing up, she would imagine the summer away playing dress-up and inventing games. The world around her was the stage and she, the actress.

"She has her dislikes, however. One of her greatest dislikes is strife. Like any family, hers had arguments, and this taught Lisa the importance of communication, collaboration, and forgiveness. Another of Lisa's dislikes is weeding. Her family had many gardens, and the whole family would work together to maintain them. Weeding helped shape her character by perseverance and dedication to see a small job, even a distasteful one, through to the end. That philosophy will last a lifetime.

"As you grow older, you learn more about life. Everything I've already mentioned about Lisa's family played a role in shaping her character into what it is today. Because of her family's dynamics, she learned the importance of honesty, even though it can be difficult. She also learned that whomever she surrounded herself with would influence her, either for good or bad.

"Decisions have consequences. Lisa learned this in many aspects, whether it be choosing not to do homework or choosing to stay home from a fun event to finish an assignment. The consequences of her decisions weren't always easy, and she had to learn to accept disappointment. There were times when she handled this disappointment poorly, which only caused more trouble. Still, these were moments that were separating her strengths from her weaknesses.

"I'd say Lisa has come a long way. She's matured beyond her 18 years, but she's not perfect. Lisa has a thirst for knowledge; however, sometimes she allows a lack of self-discipline to get in the way of achieving excellence. At other times, the seeming complexity of projects intimidates her. In spite of all this, God is gracious.

"What she lacks in some areas, she makes up for in others. God has given Lisa a heart to serve. God has also given her a joyful spirit that spreads to others. She sees the glass as half-full. Her biggest strength is her faith in God. She gives him the glory for what she does right, and she thanks Him for correction in her failures. Proverbs 12:1 says, 'Whoever loves instruction, loves knowledge.' Lisa wants to be taught."

Would someone really say these things? Maybe. It all depends on how I have lived my life. However, hearing a monologue like that would encourage me to be better.

What I appreciate about this student's response is her honesty and humility. Lisa recognizes both her strengths and her weaknesses, and she is willing to learn from her mistakes. As a teacher, this is the kind of student I would want in my own class. In fact, she has had no problem getting into the college of her choice.

YOUR CURTAIN CHOICE

Like the curtain choice on a game show, the college selection can be tough. However, don't limit your options by procrastinating. Take small steps and seek the Lord's guidance. Arm yourself with facts on your top college choices as you get advice from parents and guidance counselors. In order to keep your options open, apply early to different schools. Above all, remember that the Lord will direct your steps. It is *never* cliché to say that the Lord has a plan for your future. Just consider the college search as an exciting part of your life's adventure.

Hidden Opportunities of
Financial Aid

CHAPTER 3

Bogged down with the pressures of a full semester load and a busy job waiting tables, I asked a fellow student how she planned to make her large tuition payments. "Oh," she laughed, "I don't worry about that stuff. I'm just going to have a good time for now."

Unclear about how that actually paid her bills, I pressed further. She explained that she took out loans that would not have to be repaid until after she stopped taking classes. That did sound appealing *for the moment*, but at current college costs, that would be a graduate's nightmare.

There must be an alternative, I thought, *a better way to pay for college without burying myself under a mountain of debt*. With that thought in mind, I headed for the library. In my search, I discovered that students in the United States receive more than $105 billion in financial aid for college each year![13]

Later in my search, this small but wise ant from Proverbs 30:25 jumped out at me: "The ants are a people not strong, yet they prepare their food in the summer." I pictured the ants digging tunnels with storerooms mounding with all the crumbs they'd gathered. The ant survives by planning and hard work. Like the ant, we're called to be stewards of the time and money God has given. While I need to trust the Lord for my future, I still have a responsibility to prepare.

For many students, however, navigating the maze of financial aid is overwhelming. Fortunately, it doesn't have to be. This overview focuses on financial aid, any money that pays for college. This money comes from local and special interest groups, the student's college, state programs, and the federal government. The pie chart below illustrates how an average student packages this aid to afford college.[14]

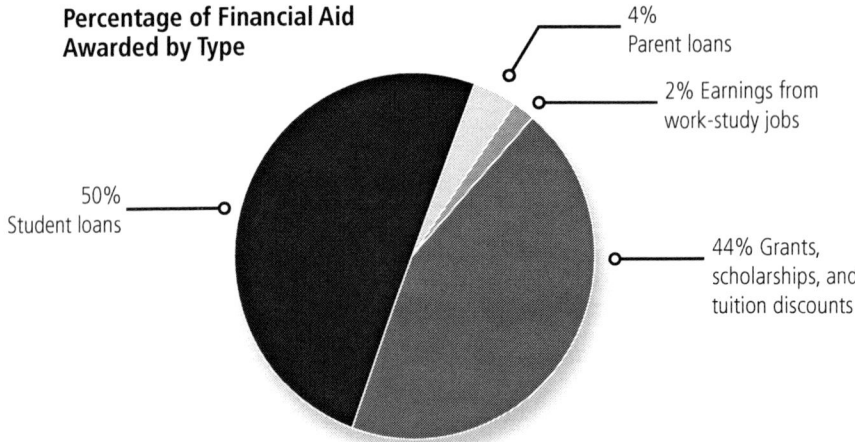

Percentage of Financial Aid Awarded by Type

- 50% Student loans
- 4% Parent loans
- 2% Earnings from work-study jobs
- 44% Grants, scholarships, and tuition discounts

Source: Minnesota Higher Education Services Office. *Financial Aid Awarded Survey* 2003.

Hopefully, 50% in student loans won't be your story. But, you may object, could I actually qualify for aid? You will, if you are dedicated to finding these opportunities. This is hard work, but persistence pays off. As one student said, "It's like a part-time job." With key information, you can receive a portion of aid money. When you feel like giving up, just research a different avenue. From personal experience, I can tell you that I was disappointed one year by the 26 rejection letters I received after applying for 30 scholarships. However, the money from the four remaining scholarships I did receive paid for a whole year of tuition and books – with money left over! The following breakdown of financial aid explains the options.

SCHOLARSHIPS

Anything free catches my attention. I quickly learned that a scholarship is free money. That's right – you don't have to pay it back. To apply for scholarships, I needed to fill out a form, occasionally write an essay, and meet specific requirements, such as special skills (i.e., musical or athletic talents) or ethnic or religious criteria. In some cases, grades and financial need were a factor. These different requirements reward students with specific characteristics. However, I was surprised to learn that there is a variety of scholarships, each catering to a specific interest, such as members of the horseshoe club, 4-H participants, basketball players, or even students with *no more* than a "C" average. Other scholarships focus specifically on minority students. In fact, there is even one scholarship available to Minnesotans who can trace their roots to a certain community in Norway!

The process of finding and applying for scholarships was somewhat time-consuming, but rewarding. In fact, I soon discovered that I had to view the process like a part-time job. I got organized and bought a file folder, which really helped.

To find scholarships, you will have to do some initial searching. Here are my suggestions:

- **Visit your local public high school.** Most high schools file scholarships, funded by local groups and donations. The school may provide a catalogue of scholarships, with requirements and deadlines. Students, from home or private school, can access these files and take appropriate applications. If you have questions regarding these applications, ask the secretary or talk with the guidance counselor.

- **Use your library's resources.** The librarian can explain the reference section on financial aid, which is updated annually. These thick books categorize scholarships into different requirements, including your home state, career choice, denomination, ethnicity, and special interests. (I highly recommend *Scholarships*, *Fellowships*, and *Loans*, published by the Gale Group.) Call, write, or e-mail the organizations listed to request an application.

- **Call or visit the financial aid office at the college.** In addition to providing scholarship information, the financial aid administrator can suggest other aid options; however, in some cases, you must be a current student in order to apply. These people work to provide information on how to make your education affordable: take advantage of this opportunity! In one case, the financial aid administrator created a package that chopped 83% off the total cost of tuition, room, and board. Your school will work with you, if do your part.

- **Contact local groups.** Many businesses and banks offer scholarships that remain unclaimed simply because there are no applicants. In fact, a firefighter reported that *not one student has ever applied* for their growing scholarship fund! Other, larger companies, such as WalMart, Target, Tylenol, and Coca-Cola, also offer aid. Don't forget to check with your parents' union or employer. Some companies, like 3M, offer scholarships to children of employees. To find other scholarship offerings in your community, glance through your local newspaper. Look for announcements of upcoming scholarship opportunities. If you notice current articles or pictures of scholarship recipients, clip these out to file and save for next year. By being alert, you will become aware of more opportunities than you initially thought.

- **Call your state's higher education services office or check their website.** In addition to a wealth of financial aid resources for your state, they will arm you with packets of information on college preparation.
- **If you're internet savvy,** check the following websites for free scholarship searches. Scholarship applications are sent to you based on your eligibility and response to basic background questions. You'll receive new applications as they are updated on the site.

    Fast Web – http://www.fastweb.com
    Free Scholarship Information – http://www.freschinfo.com
    CollegeNet Scholarship Database – http://www.collegenet.com/mach25/
    Scholarship Resource Network Express – http://www.srnexpress.com
    CollegeView – http://www.collegeview.com
    Scholarships.com – http://www.scholarships.com
    Wired Scholar Scholarship Search – http://www.wiredscholar.com/paying/

TIPS FOR SCHOLARSHIP APPLICATIONS

At first, my applications were sort of trial-and-error, but I learned some secrets. Once you find an application, take time to carefully and neatly answer all questions. Apply for anything and everything for which you qualify. Be sure you meet all the requirements. Also, some students lose money simply because they aren't looking for scholarships and don't know about the opportunities. For example, at one award ceremony I attended, the committee informed us that there was still financial aid money left in its fund because only seven applicants had responded. All seven of us received aid, and we were all invited to apply again the following year. The committee also asked us to let our friends know! At other times, applicants forego a scholarship opportunity because they are nervous or unwilling to write an essay. This type of scholarship may require a bit more time and input, but it can still pay off.

In addition, the following advice will guide you in preparing a polished and appealing request for financial aid:

- Scope out applications early. Keep a calendar and your own file system to organize scholarship applications, copies, deadlines, references, and recommendation letters.
- As with the college admissions essay, be honest, straightforward, and sincere. Any hint of overzealousness, brown-nosing, or deceit annoys the committee and is easily perceived. They know you would like the aid, but remember to be yourself.
- Be neat. If you can type or use the computer, do so. A messy application reflects poorly on you, as it is often perceived as coming from an individual who really does not care.

- Proofread for mistakes. In order to check for errors, write out your responses on a separate sheet of paper before completing the application. Read and read again to polish your responses. Then fill out your application carefully. If you do make a mistake, use correction tape or fluid.
- Check to make sure you have included all the required information: finances, test scores, references or recommendation letters, an essay or personal response, etc.
- Make a copy of everything and file it away; the same questions may show up on later applications. By making copies of recommendation letters and longer essay questions, you will save time by not repeating steps.
- Mail your fully completed application and any additional pages before the deadline, preferably early. Include proper postage!
- Be sure to send thank you letters for any recommendation letters or scholarships you receive.
- Finally, be aware of scholarship frauds. Unfortunately, some people take advantage of needy students. According to the Federal Trade Commission (FTC), be leery if:
    - You are a finalist or have won a scholarship for which you did not apply.
    - You have to pay something before you are awarded the aid.
    - The service claims that its information is unavailable elsewhere.
    - The service requests unusually personal information, like your credit card or bank account number.
    - The service guarantees money for college when you become a member.
    - Other warning signs include any fees, guarantees, broad eligibility, errors in typing or spelling, excess hype, and advertisements. If you are concerned that a scholarship service is a scam, check with you local Better Business Bureau (BBB) or call the National Fraud Information Center at 1-800-876-7060.

THE SCHOLARSHIP ESSAY

Many scholarship applications had at least one essay question, which determined whether I became a scholarship recipient. Writing a well-written response could be difficult and time-consuming, but I practiced my responses and took inventory of any accomplishments, skills, and future goals. This better equipped me to begin the application process.

To help you prepare, check out the questions below, which come from actual applications. When you do apply, be confident and write in your own unique style. It is important that your responses convey sincerity and come from your own ideas. Because many organizations may also interview you with similar questions, think carefully about how you might respond.

Academic Questions:
- What are your academic goals?
- Describe one of your academic and/or personal achievements that has given you a great sense of satisfaction or personal pride.
- Explain why your area of study interests you or discuss why you want to be a (name of your career interest).
- Describe your leadership qualities and/or participation in on-campus activities.

Financial Need Questions:
- How would this scholarship contribute to your goals?
- Briefly describe how you currently finance your education.

Career-Related Questions:
- What jobs have you held or what volunteer work have you done that might help you in your career?

Personal Character Questions:
- How do you plan to give back to the community?
- Describe your leadership qualities and/or participation in off-campus activities.
- Compose a paragraph of 50 to 100 words explaining why you believe you are deserving of this scholarship.

KEYS FOR WRITING SUCCESSFUL SCHOLARSHIP ESSAYS:
- Get to the point. Essay requirements often give a maximum word count. Choose your words carefully. Be brief!
- Be honest and sincere. Do not exaggerate accomplishments or qualities.
- Be original. Avoid clichés and other cute phrases. What qualities set you apart and make your application unique?
- Know the difference between arrogance and confidence. Understanding both your strengths and weaknesses will enable you to focus on attributes that will help your cause. For example, when writing on what qualities make you deserving of this scholarship, consider qualities like dedication, diligence, and self-motivation – not because you think you are the best candidate they'll ever see!
- Read and re-read. Any errors could disqualify you.

GRANTS

Grants are awarded through an application process, and similar to scholarships, this money does not have to be repaid. However, grants usually focus on financial need. The most important step when applying for grants is to complete the Free Application for Federal Student Aid, or FAFSA. This state grant program, based on the cost of your tuition and financial need, is awarded on a first-come, first-served basis, at an average of $1,770. Other grants and even some scholarships may require you to apply for this aid. Many colleges or universities also require that you complete the FAFSA before they will fully assist you with their financial aid package. You can apply online at www.fafsa.ed.gov no sooner than January 2 and no later than June 30 each year.

By applying for the FAFSA, you are eligible to apply for the Federal Pell Grant Program. This grant money can range anywhere from $400 to $4,000 per student. For assistance from the federal government aid hotline, call 1-800-433-3243. Government websites include <http://www.ed.gov>, <http://www.students.gov>, and <http://www.finaid.org>. To find additional grant opportunities, be aware of applications during your scholarship search.

WORK-STUDY

Your college or university offers another alternative to affording your higher education through a program called work-study. Through this option, students agree to work a part-time job throughout the year in order to help offset college costs. This work can be either on- or off-campus, but examples might include library shelving, cafeteria help, or lawn maintenance. If you do not own a vehicle, this might be a convenient option to cut down some of your tuition. Your financial aid administrator will provide more information on this option along with specific details relating to your college or university.

RECIPROCITY

Neighboring states offer students a discount by treating them as residents. For example, Minnesota exchanges reciprocity with students from Wisconsin, North and South Dakota, part of Iowa, and even the Canadian province of Manitoba. To apply for reciprocity, complete your state's online form. In many states, reciprocity automatically renews each year that the student attends classes. If you stop taking classes, you will need to reapply when you return.

GOVERNMENT SERVICE PROGRAMS

Our government hosts a variety of different options for financial aid. The Navy, Army, and Air Force all offer a full-ride, four-year scholarship in exchange for a total of nine years of service, which includes your four years of education at their academy. The Coast Guard and Merchant Marines have similar options. For a program with fewer obligations, check out the financial aid assistance of the National Guard and the Reserve Officers Training Corps (ROTC).

Other programs provide aid if you are a dependent. Under the Montgomery GI Bill, you are eligible for state and federal aid if your parent is serving in active duty. Other assistance exists if your parent served as a police officer or other government employee. In some situations, veteran benefit programs also award aid. In one scholarship application through a veteran's benefit, I received aid because my grandpa served during World War II.

TAX BENEFITS

Fortunately, some tax benefits arise while you are enrolled in school. The Hope Tax Credit allows a family to deduct up to $1,500 per student per year. A different option, the Lifetime Learning Tax Credit, subtracts up to $1,000 per student per year. However, a household may not claim both tax credits in one year. Other tax breaks include the Student Loan Interest Deduction and the Employer-Paid Tuition Assistance, each worth up to $2,500 per year. For more information, see the Internal Revenue Service website at <http://www.irs.gov/prod/forms_pubs> or call 1-800-829-3676 regarding Publication 970.

LOANS

Loans should be a last resort, taken out after a lot of thought and prayer. Several loan programs exist for students at low interest rates. However, understand the rules and read the fine print before signing. As one former student warned, "Pay attention. Keep up-to-date if your lender changes names or sells to another company. That way, you won't get confused when other lenders send you official-looking paperwork." Each loan will have a different interest rate and repayment plan. In certain situations, loans may be deferred (postponed) until students stop taking classes.

Student loans are different from other types of loans, such as personal loans on a house or car. Sure, payments may not start until after graduation, but most students consolidate, lumping all loans into one payment. Once the graduate consolidates with a lender, that lender holds the student loans until they are paid in full. This reinforces Proverbs 22:7, which states "...the borrower is servant to the lender." Unfortunately, graduate Anna Marrian discovered this principle too late: "Saddled with loans and tied to my lender for

30 years, I'm an indentured servant at 7.4 percent... I can't sell, refinance, or renegotiate my student loan, ever."[15] Little did she realize that just a few short years later, student loan interest rates would drop to their lowest point in history, a mere 1.625 percent! Interest rates today will change by graduation. Understandably, some graduates have considered filing bankruptcy. However, student loans aren't considered a valid reason for bankruptcy in the eyes of the government. The loans must still be paid in full. Failing to do so should gnaw at us as Christians because "the wicked borrows and does not pay back," according to Psalm 37:21. We should desire to take responsibility for our actions.

With that said, the following list should not serve as financial advice. However, each major loan program provided by the state and federal government is explained.

- The Federal Perkins Loan Program, offered at your university, provides up to $4,000 per year. This long-term, 5% interest loan must be repaid.

- The Federal Stafford Student Loan is available in two forms. The subsidized version requires students to meet certain criteria, while the unsubsidized version is open to all students who must repay at least the interest during school or deferment. Both types begin at $2,625, gradually working up to $5,500 for the third and fourth years. Private lenders, such as banks, offer these types of loans.

- Parents willing to pay for children's education occasionally borrow under the Federal Parent Loans for Undergraduate Students (PLUS) through private lenders. Under the PLUS program, any amount of the college cost may be borrowed with an interest rate up to 9 %. Also, repayment begins after two months.

- Students may apply for the Student Education Loan Fund (SELF) through the state's Higher Education Services Office. The interest on these long-term loans varies. For more information, see <http://www.selfloan.org>.

A FINAL WORD ON FINANCIAL AID

Do you remember that student from the beginning of this chapter? As it happened, she was unable to find a steady job after graduation. In the hopes that a higher degree would get her a better job, she returned for more classes, using more borrowed money to avoid paying back her initial loans. This is definitely not a good domino effect! As you've just discovered, that student had so many options to try before borrowing money from student loans in the first place, such as scholarships, grants, work-study, reciprocity, service programs, and tax benefits. In each of these alternatives to the student loan, a little self-motivation, planning, and hard work can be very rewarding.

Part 2 – Prepare

Dr. Huffman's Formula for Academic Success:
1. Attend your classes and take notes.
2. Read the assigned material.
3. Turn in all assignments and research papers on time.
4. Study and review every day.[16]

CHAPTER

4

Don't Just Survive, Thrive!

> Attendance at all classes is required. If you are unable to attend due to illness, please notify me beforehand. No eating, drinking, or wearing hats in class. Please turn off beepers and mobile phones before entering the classroom.
>
> The honor code is in effect at all times. Any attempt to use the work of others as your own is grounds for failing the course and expulsion from Emory. In researching and writing papers, please do not use Internet Web sites unless I have previously approved them in writing.
>
> Most Fridays will be devoted to discussing assigned readings. Read them carefully so that you are able to discuss them intelligently. Always use a dictionary to discover the meaning of words you cannot define, and keep a book of words you have learned and their definitions. I will call on you directly, by name, during class discussions.[17]

Something about that excerpt from Dr. Patrick Allitt's syllabus intrigues me. Why is it that this U.S. History professor from Emory University feels compelled to cover such basics, like following an honor code, attending class, and turning off cell phones? Doesn't it seem obvious that reading the assignments carefully in order to "discuss them intelligently" is part of a student's life at college?

Unfortunately, such "basics" are not as obvious as they used to be. Maybe that's because many students today view college as a place to clock some time, get a degree, and get on to "real life" – whatever that may be.

But college can be so much more than that. It's exciting. It's fast-paced. It prepares students for the next part of their lives. At first, the expectations and responsibilities might be a bit overwhelming, but new freedoms are also a thrill. In either case, planning, organizing, and managing time pays huge returns. As you learn how to juggle a busy schedule, you'll learn time-saving tricks. With balance, you'll also feel satisfied when you plan for both study and fun or simply hanging out with friends. In addition, you'll get more sleep and avoid getting sick. Whether or not you've developed strategies of time management and study skills, this chapter provides a solid foundation to help you thrive in college – not just survive.

FOCUS ON PRIORITIES

We all have 24 hours in a day, 168 hours in a week, and 8,736 hours in a year. Does that sound like a lot? It can be, even though the average person sleeps one-third of that time. To make the most of our time, it's important to organize activities around priorities. As Christians, our first priority is our relationship with the Lord. *Nothing* can replace the time spent in cultivating our walk with Him. Our next priority lies in one's relationship to family. People come before personal goals. Avoid being so rigid in your plans that you neglect serving and appreciating others. On the other hand, however, going to classes and being fully prepared should be a high priority at this point in your life. College life is a new change with many opportunities for involvement. It's all too easy to fill up any extra time with friends and events, leaving little room for priorities.

When it comes to college life, discernment is a learned skill. Sometimes you'll have to choose between what's necessary (like studying for midterms) and what's extra (like your friends' spontaneous idea of midnight bowling). As you prioritize, discernment helps you choose what's best.

Unfortunately, many students don't know this skill. They're lost in a whirlwind of choices offered on campus. For example, Kate, a talented senior I know, immersed herself in a schedule without *one* free evening. As weeks passed, the pressure mounted. Finally, exhausted from her obligations, Kate called her parents to help her untangle all the commitments and regain focus of her priorities.

To be most effective with your time, it's important to recognize what's necessary. Ron Fry, author of *The Great Big Book of How to Study* writes, you must,

> *Make choices about what is important to you, to help you set goals for yourself, to help you organize and schedule your time, and to develop the motivation and self-discipline to follow your schedule and reach toward those goals.*[18]

The following section will help guide you in forming both long- and short-term plans.

FIGURE OUT YOUR ROAD MAP

Cut pressure by planning ahead. The beauty of schedules is that they "serve as a concrete reminder of tasks, events, due dates, responsibilities, and deadlines."[19] A schedule will also help you meet goals. During my junior year, I stumbled upon a highly effective tool for scheduling. I only wish I had known of it earlier. As simple as it may sound, this easy technique enabled me to spread out challenging essays and projects during down times – not during hectic midterms and finals. Aside from using this technique in school, I've also found its principles helpful for planning long-term goals in my daily living.

So what's this technique? On the first day of each class, get a syllabus from the professor. The syllabi should explain each professors' classroom expectations, grading policies, and semester plan, outlining any major essays, research papers, or exams. Read the syllabi carefully. They will form a road map for your semester. By plotting out important dates on a time line or calendar, you will be able to predict where your personal "crunch times" will take place. You can then plan ahead to work on required reading or research papers that fall around hot spots, like midterms and finals. This is important because, as Associate Professor Gary Morgan from Northwestern College said, "Few professors are willing to let you turn in an assignment late because, 'I didn't look at the syllabus.'"[20]

For example, Stephanie, a first-semester junior taking 15 units (or credits), successfully used this system to organize her long- and short-term projects. On the following page, Stephanie's calendar enables her to visualize the overall picture for the semester.

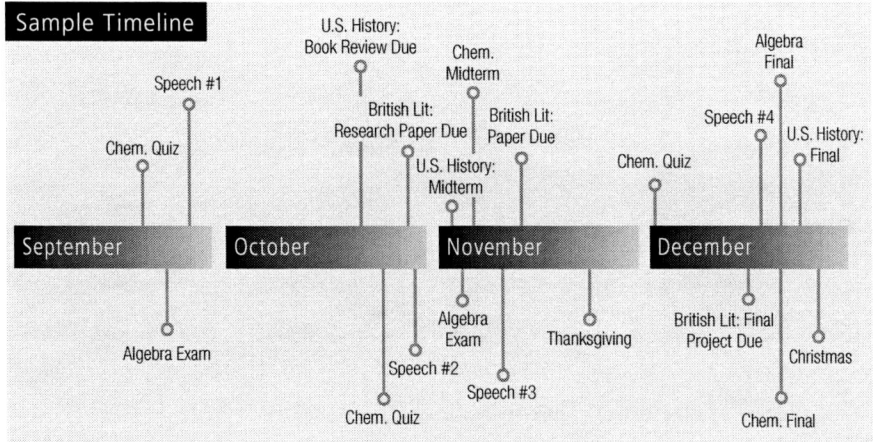

Creating such a time line allows Stephanie to see long-term projects over one semester. As you can see, the end of October through the beginning of November will be rather intense study times for her, as well as the end of the semester in mid-December. Through careful planning, however, Stephanie can form short-term steps based on her long-term goals. For example, she can read the book for U.S. History and write her review during her spare time after her first speech. This will free up her time to begin work on the British Literature research paper early, in order to have as much time as possible to study and prepare for midterms. This same strategy and foresight can be used throughout the semester for her additional projects due near the end of the semester.

However, in planning and carrying out a schedule, take note of the following tips:

- **Identify your peak study time.** Ideally, the time you're most alert should be used for studies. By recognizing these times during the day, you'll be more prepared mentally to attack the books. Down time could better be used on less mentally draining activities, like doing laundry or cleaning your dorm room.
- **Plan ahead.** Although planning takes time and effort, you won't regret the energy you spend getting into a routine.
- **Be realistic about your goals.** Each student works at his own pace. You have no one to compete against but yourself, and for some, this is all the pressure that's needed. Push yourself to succeed, but accept your limitations.
- **Avoid procrastination.** There are two helpful steps in avoiding procrastination: first, break a large project into smaller, more manageable pieces. Second, tackle the most overwhelming part of the project while you're still fresh. This accomplishment will feed your motivation to continue.
- **Pace yourself.** Don't burn yourself out by pulling all-night cram fests, which leave you on a major low after the caffeine and sugar has worn off. When test time arrives, you won't be able to think clearly anyway. In a few pages, we'll cover some suggestions for studying for tests.
- **Don't over-schedule.** Leave time for unplanned fun. Scheduling gaps release pressure and refresh your mind between obligations.
- **Avoid time traps, but be flexible.** People come first. However, learn to say no at times to those extras that eat your time and spend your energy.
- **Evaluate your progress.** Review your goals occasionally. By monitoring your progress, you will stay focused and on schedule.

These simple techniques prepare you with a relaxed yet focused mindset in college. Because you've taken the crucial time to plan a schedule designed around your semester, you'll feel more balanced, motivated, and energetic. This preparation enables you to thrive both in the classroom and on your own, if you study consistently.

TAKE GOOD NOTES

Today, we use technology to communicate. We like instant messages and shortcuts to conversation, like LOL and RUOK. Maybe you even use symbols to convey emotions, like :-) for happy and :-o for surprise. Just as these time-saving techniques are useful in e-mails and text messages, shorthand is perfect for taking notes.

However, students need the basic tools. The thought of entering a college classroom with a professor who lectures for an hour and a half straight can be scary, unless you're trained in following along and taking notes.

Before you begin, understand that professors vary widely in how they present material. Some may hold in-class activities, like small group discussions, while others lecture for the entire period and only occasionally scribble notes on a board. Still other professors present notes from an overhead projector or PowerPoint presentation. No matter which style your instructor prefers, train your mind to look for the essence, or the main idea. Only then can you connect personal experiences and examples to this main idea.

To begin taking notes, use a clear and personalized system. Start a new page with the day's date at the beginning of each lecture. Here's an example. Make two columns in your notebook by drawing a vertical line about one-third of the way in from the left side. The larger section to the right will be used for in-class notes, while the smaller section on the left will be used later to identify key terms, names, and dates or to jot down study questions. You can then use this smaller, left column as a quick guide when you review and study for an exam.

To take notes quickly and efficiently, you don't want to write down *everything*. Jot down key phrases, terms and definitions, people, events, and dates. Watch for important numbers, facts, percentages, and formulas. Familiarize yourself with the following symbols and their definitions, but also consider using your own code or system of abbreviations. Although you may already use common symbols like #, &, %, and $, you may want to adapt some of these into your own notes:

Symbol	Definition
*	Take Note
^	Insert
@	At
w/	With
w/o	Without
etc.	Et cetera; and so on
e.g. or i.e.	For example
b/c	Because

In addition, become familiar with standard acronyms, initials, and fractions. If you don't understand a symbol that your professor uses, ask! In a history class during my senior year, one professor repeatedly drew a large "x" in the middle of his chalkboard. Finally, it dawned on me that whenever he made this symbol, he was saying the word *against*. For example, the colonists fought *against* the British. I would have saved myself a lot of confusion if I had initially asked what he meant. This same rule especially applies to composition classes where your professor may use a shorthand system of abbreviations to correct your papers. If you never ask what those symbols mean, you may never improve your writing style.

HOW DO YOU LEARN BEST?

Each person has developed a learning style that meets his needs best. In fact, whether they realize it or not, most people have even created study patterns. For example, one friend of mine can only fully concentrate if he is sitting in a quiet, brightly lit room with a pencil sharpener nearby. However, another friend has grown so accustomed to ignoring background noise while studying that he must turn on some music or the TV in order to focus. Whether or not you can relate to either of these two, you most likely have established your own habits of study. The following quiz, entitled "My Ideal Study Environment" from *The Great Big Book of How to Study* offers an excellent guide to determine how, when, and where you study best.

Your ideal study environment may be completely different from your best friend's. Keep in mind, however, that each person learns most effectively according to his own learning style, needs, and habits. For example, your friend might find it ideal to study in her quiet dorm room, while you prefer an active coffee shop. There is nothing wrong with this, as long as you can truly focus and accomplish your tasks. Understanding these differences should also make you more sensitive to a roommate whose ideal study environment greatly differs from your own. Avoid cranking up the stereo when your roommate is trying to study in peace.

How I receive information best:
1. ___ Orally   ___ Visually

In the classroom, I should:
2. ___ Concentrate on taking notes   ___ Concentrate on listening
3. ___ Sit in front ___ Sit in back ___ Sit near window or door

Where I study best:
4. ___ At home ___ In the library ___ Somewhere else: _____

When I study best:
5. ___ Every night; little on weekends ___ Mainly on weekends
   ___ Spread out over seven days
6. ___ In the morning ___ Evening ___ Afternoon
7. ___ Before dinner ___ After dinner

How I study best:
8. ___ Alone ___ With a friend ___ In a group
9. ___ Under time pressure ___ Before I know I have to
10. ___ With music ___ In front of TV ___ In a quiet room
11. ___ Organizing an entire night's studying before I start
    ___ Tackling and completing one subject at a time

I need to take a break:
12. ___ Every 30 minutes ___ Every hour ___ Every 2 hours
    ___ Every _____ hours [21]

GATHER YOUR MATERIALS

When you study, make the most of your time by being fully prepared. Now that you can identify your ideal study environment, gather any materials and find a place that helps you concentrate. Depending on noise, times of day, or other distractions, choose more than one study area that lets you focus. The following are suggestions to consider as you gather these materials and establish a routine:

- **Do you have everything you need?** Check your stash of pens, paper, handouts, class notes, personal reading notes, textbooks, computer access, and possibly a beverage.

- **Do you have proper lighting?** If you own or use a computer, does the screen face a sunny window? (If it's hard to see, you might be straining your eyes over time.)
- **Is your workspace organized to avoid unnecessary distractions?** Avoid fumbling through messy stacks of paper and desk supplies by setting up a simple file system and supply station.
- **Are you working to avoid distractions?** You might need to unplug the phone, click out of chat rooms or e-mail, or hang a "Please Do Not Disturb" sign on the knob.
- **Do you have the right chair?** Try to choose one comfortable – yet not so cozy that you are sure to doze off!

DOWN TO BUSINESS

Now that you're fully prepared, it's time to focus. The key to effective study lies all in your approach. As Brian Marshall's book title suggests, *Study Smarter, Not Harder*.

As you prepare for exams, midterms, and finals, adopt the mindset that your education is not just a letter grade. You should desire to make the most of your education by allowing this experience to impact your life. With that in mind, apply yourself to your studies by carefully considering and evaluating what you learn.

> *Approach your test preparation as an active, critical thinker, working to understand material rather than just to repeat facts. As you study, try to connect ideas to examples, analyze cause and effects, establish truths, and look at issues from different perspectives.*[22]

Review all of your notes from class and your readings. Sort through information and weed out anything extra, such as background information. Then refer back to your textbook and review the major headings. This will refocus your mind on the chapter's organization. You may find the following study tips helpful as well:

- **Concentrate on the topic.** Remain interested and focused.
- **Avoid cramming.** Last-minute attempts to learn material fail because information is only stored in short-term memory, which is easily forgotten.
- **Make connections to your own life.** Try to associate what you're learning with what you already know. This connection forms a bridge, which helps you truly remember because it is now stored in your long-term memory. The more information you link to your own experiences, the easier your study preparation and actual testing will be.

- **Start at the general and move to the specific.** In memorizing, "Study the big picture, then learn the details. Learning and memorizing are like a funnel – the process is not very effective when the small end is at the top."[23]

- **Construct a concept map,** which centers on the main ideas and branches out to subpoints and supporting details or examples. Creating such a map prepares you to identify what is important and organize your own thoughts.

- **Create a visual picture.** Many people learn better through pictures. Visualize a scene of what you are learning or design a grid, map, chart, stick figure, or simple illustration to help remind you of the bigger picture.

- **Simplify larger points into one key word or phrase.** The abbreviated form of the concept enables you to memorize and recall items in a series more quickly and efficiently.

MEMORY TECHNIQUES

With these principles to focus our approach to studying successfully, we now turn to specific memory techniques, or mnemonic devices. Again, your goal is to capture the essence of the material, then the supporting details. These tools enable you to retrieve information quickly because they are associated with familiar ideas or pictures.

- **Flashcards** – Using flashcards teaches students to identify and define key terms and concepts. Because they're compact, you can easily carry these cards around and study them any time – like when you're waiting for your laundry to dry. However, the potential problem with flashcards lies in their repetitive approach to learning key facts and details. Since your brain categorizes information differently (long-term as opposed to short-term memory), you will study more effectively by making connections to the facts and details you memorize. The next time you use flashcards, try using a related picture next to the term. You'll probably remember the information easier because you can associate the term with a visual aid.

- **Acronyms** – Most of us know that Roy G. Biv is not the name of some eccentric scientist. Instead, we recognize these letters as the initials for the colors of the rainbow: red, orange, yellow, green, blue, indigo, and violet. Use acronyms to remember your own list of terms easily.

- **Strange Sentences** – Similar to acronyms, strange sentences use the first letter of each concept or term to remember and create a sentence. For example, you might recall "every good boy does fine" as the notes on the treble clef line. Using the same technique, my eighth-grade science teacher taught me the names of the planets through the following sentence: "My very educated mother just sold us nine pizzas." Of course, the order of the planets corresponds as Mercury, Venus, Earth, Mars, Jupiter, Saturn, Uranus, Neptune, and Pluto. This technique became quite helpful in chemistry and physics later.

- **Songs** – Have you ever needed to memorize a longer list or sentence that couldn't be condensed? Try linking those words with a song you already know. My fourth grade history class learned all of the presidents in order to the tune of "William Tell's Overture," better known as the theme song for "The Lone Ranger." To this day, I still remember our presidents in order!

- **Rhyme Time** – Most likely, you know the popular line, "In 1492, Columbus sailed the ocean blue." Another example is the familiar spelling rule: "I before E, except after C, or when saying A, as in neighbor and weigh. Four exceptions if you please: *either, neither, seizure, seize.*" The simple technique of rhyming links facts and information in a memorable way.

Mnemonic devices work by making information meaningful and accessible. The facts are associated with what is already known or familiar to us, enabling us to remember information longer and more clearly. As you study in preparation for your next test, practice some of these techniques until they become habits.

In addition to using mnemonic devices for a test, other techniques enable you to make the most of your time, energy, and resources. Pre-test your knowledge of the material. Record questions on a tape and listen while running errands or exercising. How well can you remember and apply the information you have learned? If an exam requires the use of formulas, how comfortable are you when practicing these in different problems? As a final suggestion, form study groups. Quiz each other and compare notes or examples to learn more from other perspectives. As you practice these study suggestions, you will feel much more prepared and relaxed when test time arrives.

TAKING THE TEST

As you prepare for your next test, try to find out how the instructor will be testing. Common forms of testing fall under one of two categories: objective or subjective. Objective tests seek short, one-word or one-phrase answers to test your recall on information. These tests include true or false statements, multiple choice, terms to match, or short answer. While subjective tests seek the same information, you may also be challenged to organize, process, and expand upon the facts using critical thinking. A typical example of a subjective test is the essay response. Although some professors use a combination of both types of testing, you can prepare better if you know the style of the test beforehand.

Tips for an Objective Test:

- **Read all the directions carefully.** There may be more than one step in the section, or your instructor may require a specific style, such as the use of capital letters in your answers because they are easier to read and grade.

- **Completely read** any lists, questions, or choice selections before you answer.

- **Answer what you know** (or what is easiest) first. Return to more difficult problems or questions later.

- **Watch for precise words** like *not*, *always*, *never*, and *all*. Qualifiers like *usually*, *sometimes*, and *occasionally* bring exceptions to extremes.

- **In matching,** eliminate answers you do know first, and cross these out – except if answers can be used more than once.

Tips for a Subjective Test:

- **Read the directions thoroughly.** Watch for key words like *compare* and *contrast*, *evaluate*, *prove*, *define*, or *summarize*. These key words clue you in to the actions you must take and the appropriate form of your response.

- **Before writing**, create a brief outline or map of the main idea and supporting details. This will guide you and allow you to make adjustments before writing your response.

- **In your first sentence**, rephrase the question in your own words as an introduction to your main points.

- **Provide any strong supporting details**, evidence, examples, or personal reactions, as required in the directions.

- **Read your completed response** and correct any errors in content, grammar, or mechanics.

No matter what type of test you are taking, use critical thinking to help you form the best answers and avoid mistakes. Keep an eye on the clock, but don't focus on it. If you've studied diligently, you can relax in the knowledge that you have truly done your best. Try to be positive. Your instructor tests your knowledge and ability to relay information in order to discover what you know. The professor desires your success in learning and applying information – not just scoring a good grade.

FOR ASPIRING UNDERGRADS

Success as a student requires the right mindset to focus your energy on what is important and to organize your time into a well-ordered but flexible schedule. As you prepare to soak up the most from the college experience, understand that education is what you make of it. Embrace the love of learning for its own sake, and respect the student-teacher relationship. In the classroom, develop an organized, personal system of note taking – regardless of the style in which the information is delivered. On your own, mentally engage in the text by investigating the main idea and making connections to life. In preparing for the test, try out the suggestions to see what works for you. The thoughtful student approaches the complete college experience as an exciting opportunity to learn and grow as a person. By cultivating a balanced approach to your studies, you too will learn to thrive – not just survive!

Communicate in the
Classroom

CHAPTER

5

Have you ever seen a clip of Ebert and Roper? These critics discuss their views on recent movies, indicating approval by "thumbs up." In their reviews, they talk about specific features of a movie, such as theme, characterization, setting, style, and plot. Most professors expect that college students will be able to read and discuss a text in a similar manner, but discussing what you've read is more than just a quick critique with a commercial break.

Of course, a key step toward class discussion is actually reading the assignment. If you really want to take part in discussion, though, you'll need to go beyond restating what you've read. You'll need to *ask questions* to expand and develop points in the text. You'll also need to support ideas with *specific examples* from the reading and compare the information to other issues. Specifically, you'll need to *make connections* and *add personal feedback*. In other words, "we need an approach to reading which not only tells us what an author said, but also why he said it, whether what he said is true, and what the worth of his contribution is."[24] At times, you'll need to go further than what's required, to think about how the topic relates to God's standards. This may take some extra effort on your part, especially if you research what others have written on the topic, but it'll be well worth your time. Through this process, you might discover that your convictions are more solid. You'll also be able to communicate your ideas and beliefs more effectively.

GETTING THE MOST FROM YOUR TEXTBOOK

College assignments usually include large amounts of reading. Your ability to read comprehensively and find the main ideas saves time and energy when you study. If you're going to fully comprehend, though, you need to prepare.

This starts with getting your mind ready *before* you read. Focus on the ideas in the book and follow the author's train of thought. When reading, try to guess what the next point might be. Comprehension is the foundation of learning.

- **Before You Read** – Besides preparing the mind, specific tools will help you understand the assignment. First, be sure you completely understand the assignment. Then preview the text by checking out any headings, sub-headings, or other words typed in bold or italics. This will give you a better feel for the text's structure and organization. You may also find a summary of important points at the end of the chapter. If you read the summary first, you'll be able to pick out the main points easily when reading.

- **While You Read** – Perhaps the most simple, yet often overlooked part of reading is being invested in the content. Sometimes it's hard to concentrate. You might even find yourself reading and rereading the same sentence. This is both a frustration and a waste of time. Train your mind to focus by identifying the main idea. When you concentrate on that main idea, you can make connections to supporting points and examples. Study any maps, charts, graphs, and pictures. These visual aids usually develop the point, which helps when you review.

In some cases, you may struggle to simply understand the ideas in a text. When this happens, break the section into smaller pieces. Read one paragraph at a time, then write in the margin a phrase or short sentence to capture the main idea of that paragraph.

The strategy of using context clues can help you capture the idea of a passage by using nearby or related words in the text. Such context clues appear as synonyms, comparisons and contrasts, definition or description, words in a series, cause and effect, and examples.[25] Other clues include transitional words, which signal a directional change to a different or supporting idea. Examples of these transitional words or phrases might include *consequently*, *in contrast*, *as a result*, *however*, *for instance*, *although*, and *furthermore*. Be aware of these changes as they reveal the main ideas and supporting elements of a text.

Of course, always use a dictionary for difficult words and study guides, like *Spark Notes* or *Cliff Notes*. Even though these tips take more time, they will help you later because you'll be more engaged with the text and retain more information while reading.

Many students develop the habit of writing in their books to focus on important points. They'll highlight or use numbers, dashes, checks, exclamation points, and stars. Also, take notes while reading to remember details, points, page numbers, key quotes, and other information. However, if these tips don't appeal to you, consider using that left column (under "Study Skills") from your class notes to identify key ideas, ask questions, and record page numbers from the book. When you've finished reading, your notes will form a personal study guide.

Train your mind to ask questions while reading. After a while, you may develop your own specific questions for each type of text, but the following questions will help you get started:
- What's the main idea of this chapter or section?
- What examples are provided?
- What is the next logical step in the process?
- How does this content compare or contrast with another authority on the topic?
- How does this information add to my understanding or change my perspective on the issue?

Answering these questions helps you track with the author and connect to the text. This makes learning more meaningful.

○ **After You Read –** When you're finished reading and taking notes, always review the main idea and its supporting points. Since you've taken notes, you now have a guide by which to study. If you train yourself to do a quick review of these notes after reading, you'll discover that you remember more *later*.

READING FOR DISCUSSION

Your instructors may add other books, short stories, or poetry to your regular textbook reading, followed by class discussion. Some students dread discussion, though. They simply don't know where to begin or what to say. Each minute passes painfully, and they can't wait until the end of the hour. For other students, however, the classroom suddenly becomes alive; it's thought provoking, a great place to toss around ideas and join meaningful conversations.

No matter which group you can relate to, you can gain a lot from this experience. It's important to know how to approach this process, though. The following steps offer some ideas for getting the most out of discussion in the college classroom.

1) Summarize – If you don't understand the book, you won't be able to discuss it well, elaborate on its significance, or add to your own understanding. This first step is crucial as it lays the groundwork for the rest of your critique. Based largely on the summary, a reader will choose to either accept or reject the ideas or take a new course of action altogether. Use the following questions to help you get started:

- What is the purpose of the article or chapter?
- What are the key issues or main ideas?
- What details and examples are used?
- What new vocabulary and definitions have been presented?

 2) Reflect – You've probably heard the old saying, "Think before you speak." We should also take the time to think before we react. Each of us has different experiences that help us approach literature from different angles. Reflection gives us a chance to consider an issue before we respond.

 3) Analyze – In order to understand a concept better, we need to break down that concept into smaller, more manageable pieces. Analysis examines the details by classifying, mapping, comparing and contrasting, creating character sketches, forming patterns of cause and effect, or establishing connections to other people, places, events, or ideas. For example, to analyze Odysseus' character traits in *The Odyssey*, you might first map out the different places to which Odysseus traveled. You would then be able to categorize which traits he modeled at each site. Other approaches might be to compare Odysseus to other minor characters or to explain the cause and effect of Odysseus' actions. Analysis gives us flexibility in how we approach a topic, while still providing a concrete approach to analyzing literature.

 4) Interpret – At this point, you'll need to respond to what you've read. Of course, the way you respond to the ideas in a book will influence whether you accept or reject that book. The key to interpreting, however, is basing your opinions on specific examples or reasonable implications from the text. In other words, you need to support your ideas with proof. Before you accept or reject an idea, though, Dr. Leland Ryken gives the following points on responding to literature in his book, *Triumphs of the Imagination*:

- It is possible to respond positively to a work whose view of reality we consider untruthful but whose artistry we find magnificent.
- It is possible that our antipathy to a work's view of reality will destroy our enjoyment of the work.
- We can enjoy a work whose artistic quality is poor or mediocre but whose intellectual content grips us powerfully.
- It is possible to agree with the viewpoint of a work yet respond unfavorably to its lack of artistry.[26]

 Reading and responding to literature requires balance, which shows maturity in acknowledging what is beautiful or artistic about a work without accepting what is ugly, unimaginative, or untruthful. We can enjoy the good elements in a work, such as the style, while opposing the ideas which do not value or mirror God's truths.

5) Evaluate – Assessment, a final measure of a piece of literature, considers all factors to evaluate or judge its worth. Keep in mind, though, that content is more important than form. *What* is written is more important than *how* it is written, which means you'll need to focus mainly on a work's logic, clarity, accuracy, and effectiveness. The following questions make great tools for evaluation:

- What are this text's strengths and weaknesses?
- Is the style effective and captivating?
- Is this section clear, accurate, and truthful?
- Is this text logical and meaningful?
- After defining, analyzing, and interpreting the text, what is the overall value or worth of this piece?

Just as Christians need to evaluate situations in daily life by God's standards, you'll need to weigh the ideas in a text by God's truths. Only then will you be able to assess accurately the claims that the text makes to truth and reality. As James Williams points out, "If there is little to evaluate morally or rationally, we are still free to appreciate what is beautiful." However, he writes, "The greatest art is true, skillfully expressed, imaginative, and unencumbered by the personal and emotional hang-ups of its originators."[27]

This process of literary criticism allows us to evaluate literature, reject false information, and identify what's of value. There is a word of warning, however, in all of this reading and discussing of literature. Sometimes we can go too far in our attempts to interpret or evaluate a text. G.K. Chesterton, a critic during the 1800s, wrote about this problem after reading the responses made by literary critics on Lewis Carroll's *Alice's Adventures in Wonderland*:

> *I am sorry to say it, but the soap bubble which poor old Dodgson blew from the pipe of poetry, in a lucid interval of lunacy, and sent floating into the sky, has been robbed by educationists of much of the lightness of the bubble, and retained only the horrible healthiness of the soap.*[28]

In Chesterton's view, over-analysis destroyed anything that could have been fun. It's my hope that this process of reading will help you to think more critically and evaluate what you read. Although this process may not always be *required*, it's always important to think about the ideas beneath the surface. Whether those ideas take shape in a textbook, a story, or a poem, how do they measure?

The guiding question in research is 'so what?'
Answer that question in every sentence you write.

– Donald W. McClosky[29]

CHAPTER

6

Rave Reviews on the
Research Paper

MEANINGFUL RESEARCH

One semester, I was surprised when even my math professor, Dr. David Sammons, required a research paper! For this reason, Dr. Sammons said, "If you can explain an equation in words, then you can prove that you really understand the material."

During my time at college, I continued to find that professors frequently use writing to measure a student's knowledge of a subject. For many students, however, this is bad news. It's hard to communicate ideas if you don't know where to start or what to say.

But wait! There's hope for the reluctant research writer. If you are one who dreads this process, you may want to rethink your concept of research. Don't view the finished product as just a grade. An opportunity to research offers a chance to learn a subject well and create something new from your perspective. The better you learn to research now, the easier it will be during college when your time is more limited.

To get started, let's explore what a research paper involves. The goal of any research project is either to expose information or to stir the reader to some new thought or response. Research writing presents ideas. Fresh, original, and creative points catch a reader's attention, but a research paper can also draw from initially borrowed ideas. Your knowledge of the subject will develop as you find more information on your topic. The key here is that supporting evidence strengthens *your own ideas*.

This does not require you to "reinvent the wheel," though. We can't experience *everything* first-hand. At times, we must rely on others for information. By finding reliable sources, you can skillfully frame and develop your points. Research allows us to explore ideas, refine our understanding of a subject, and communicate this knowledge to others. To support ideas, use outside evidence. As you write, ask yourself, "Am I clear, accurate, and unbiased as I communicate this information?"

This makes a research paper much different from an opinion essay. While an opinion lacks documented evidence, ideas are still expressed. In contrast, a research paper supports ideas with direct evidence. Potentially, this can move readers to new thoughts, responses, or action. Direct evidence can include facts, data, eyewitness reports, charts, and graphs – anything to grab the reader's attention. Just remember to document any borrowed proof. "By citing sources in your essays or reports, you merely show your readers that you have investigated your ideas and found support for them. In addition, using sources affords your readers the opportunity to look into your subject further if they so desire, consulting your references for further information."[30] Including sources adds credibility to your ideas. Just be sure to explain the relevance of these ideas.

A research paper is not just a gathering of references, nor is it a summary of many people's ideas. Instead, the challenge of a research paper is for a writer to evaluate ideas and either propose a new way of looking at a subject or further develop an existing topic. The writer needs to make the connection from ideas to supporting evidence. Outside sources add credibility and boost a writer's points. If you keep an open mind, this can be an exciting and eye-opening experience as you continue learning how to communicate your own ideas. Remember, the better you can write *before* college, the easier your experience *during* college.

PLAN YOUR APPROACH

Have you ever thought about what goes into a commercial? There's the subliminal message, the appeal to emotions, the characters, the lighting, the music – oh, yes, and there's the product. When we actually sit down to think about what we've seen, it's amazing to discover how much information can be packed into 20 or 30 seconds.

We can learn a lot from a commercial's package. Because of the speed at which these ideas are thrown out, it's not typical to really *question* the information. There's no time! We aren't required to support our ideas with reliable, relevant evidence – let alone communicate these ideas in a coherent piece of writing. Maybe that's why so many students shudder at the thought of research. Other hurdles include a lack of motivation, experience, knowledge, or skills.

Only you can change your approach to research. If you don't know where to start because you lack experience or information, this next section will give you some direction. The deeper you jump into a topic, the more invested you'll become and the more you'll be able to verbalize your ideas through writing. This becomes a powerful motivation to learn.

To get you started, gather all the relevant books and articles you can find. What evidence do you need to support your ideas? Three common research strategies help the writer expose and communicate ideas.

1) Divide and Conquer – Separate and examine the smaller parts of a topic to find out how those parts relate to the big picture. Analysis involves a close examination of the details. In a research paper, this means exploring the reasons or evidence that supports the main idea. In other words, investigate, ask questions, and study.

2) Put It Back Together – Synthesis reconnects those parts, showing the relationships between ideas. In a research paper, this brings a new or unique approach to looking at a subject. It makes connections between ideas and supporting evidence. You end up creating something new or redesigning an old topic.

3) Weigh the Evidence – Most important to the research paper, you'll need to evaluate what you've studied by offering some kind of feedback or judgment. Determine the relevance of the information to the main idea before you respond, then be sure to include specific examples to support your evaluation.

If you're not used to supporting your ideas with evidence, these strategies might be difficult. However, these skills train our minds to think from a fresh perspective.

Key questions also direct research efforts. Use the following questions as a guide when beginning your paper:

- Have I gathered as much information as I can on this subject before writing?
- Have I studied all angles of the issue in order to present this topic accurately? Do I know all the facts and understand opposing points of view?
- How can I organize my ideas to make sense? Does each supporting piece of evidence point back to the main idea?
- What fresh perspective, new insight, or change of focus can I bring to give this topic new life and meaning?
- How can I combine this information with what I already know?

Such questions give us an opportunity to reflect upon our ideas as we provide supporting evidence. No longer do we simply plug in a quote to take up space and meet the minimum requirements of the paper. Instead, ideas can be thoughtfully expanded and developed. Research suddenly takes on new meaning.

STUDY THE SKELETON

If you are going to write well, it's important to understand the parts that make up a research paper. Just as a skeleton provides a framework for the body, specific elements provide a framework for a solid research paper. Study these elements before you begin the writing process.

1) Topic – The topic is the subject on which you focus. Your instructor may assign a topic, or you may have the freedom to choose your own. In either case, fully invest yourself to make this a rich and meaningful project. Readers will notice your enthusiasm. Give the project relevance by connecting it to your own life. If the topic is assigned, consider how it might relate to your previous experiences, to your current studies or interests, or to your future concerns. If the topic is your choice, pick something of genuine interest – something that's not redundant, obvious, or worn out by overuse. Be original and unique.

Carefully consider the extent of your topic. Don't limit yourself by making the topic too narrow. It will be difficult to find enough material to support your ideas. In contrast, a topic that's too broad can be just as challenging. You'll be bombarded by information, which can make the project overwhelming and complicated. To avoid either of these extremes, do a simple check for outside sources before you commit to that topic.

2) Thesis – A thesis serves as a clear, concise statement of purpose to express the main idea of your paper. This crucial statement acts as a single guiding force to direct your research through supporting evidence. While reminding *you* of the purpose for your project, it also serves as a guide for your *readers*. Your goal should be to inform them, focusing their attention on what makes your approach significant and unique. "When you write with others in mind, you give your ideas the critical attention they need and deserve. You disentangle them from your memories and wishes, so that you – and others – can explore, expand, combine, and understand them more fully."[31]

Of course, remember that such a statement is a work in progress. Do not expect your thesis statement to be in its final form at the start of the project. As you gather your evidence and supporting details, you may need to slightly readjust your focus and tweak your thesis to state the purpose more accurately. In some situations, you may need to completely revise the sentence so that it fits the new direction of your paper. As one writer warned, "Don't try to pass off an old head on the body of a new statue!"[32] However, make sure that your revised thesis still meets the guidelines for the assignment.

Typically, the thesis is found in the first or second paragraph as an introduction to your paper. It should focus on one specific idea, united with your clear, directly expressed opinion. Don't just ask a question or state the controversy in your topic and plow into the paper. For the reader, the whole purpose is to learn something new through your fresh perspective. Capture your reader's attention immediately by being direct, confident, and clear.

I've emphasized the point that a thesis is part subject and part opinion. However, you should be careful to use logic and make sense in the thesis. Don't oversimplify the issue or belittle those who might object. An excellent thesis lays a natural foundation for the supporting evidence and explanation to follow.

3) Perspective – A persuasive research paper is only convincing with a solid claim, clear points, and specific, supporting evidence. In your topic, what is the situation? Where are you coming from? Lay this foundation in your introduction. However, avoid prejudices, bias, and pure emotionalism. You can do this by using supporting evidence throughout the paper.

Clearly identify your audience. "You will understand your own work better when you try to anticipate your readers' questions:

- How have you evaluated your evidence?
- Why do you think it is relevant?
- How do your claims add up?
- What ideas have you considered but rejected?
- How can you respond to your readers' predictable questions, reservations, and objections?"[33]

As you seek to inform or persuade your readers effectively, consider their questions or concerns. The *manner* in which you convey your ideas will make all the difference.

Never shy away from truth. Instead, work to develop the skills to clearly communicate your ideas and proof. Make clear connections between thoughts, reasons, and evidence. Most importantly, evaluate your reasons and evidence fairly. Acknowledge different points of view, and recognize exceptions where necessary. This reveals the balance, accuracy, and attention to details that you should desire to convey through your writing.

4) Supporting Evidence – In order to make a valid claim or hold a meaningful argument, you must provide truthful and dependable evidence. Examples include personal experiences, testimonials, analogies, comparison-contrasts, case studies, detailed descriptions, factual data, and visual aids, such as diagrams, tables, charts, and graphs.

Whenever you use another's ideas, work to accurately relay and assess the information. Ask questions.

- What did the source state or imply?
- What examples *from the material* can I find to explain my interpretation of the material?

Just as you would not appreciate your statements being misquoted or misinterpreted, you need to be careful in your writing to use quotes fairly and in context. Look at the words, phrases, or passages surrounding a quote or idea to understand its full meaning. Be aware of a writer's sarcasm, use of humor, or irony to prove a point. Never fabricate, distort, or knowingly misrepresent your sources to suit your own expectations or beliefs. If you evaluate your sources fairly, you'll learn more as the information adds to or changes your current ideas.

Of course, to use evidence effectively, you must be able to recognize the difference between fact and opinion. A fact is a provable piece of evidence. An opinion, however, is based on a personal judgment or evaluation of a subject, which hinges on beliefs, ideas, or concepts. An opinion may or may not rely on accurate proof. It's important to understand this difference as we examine sources and use evidence in our writing.

In addition, we need to have a balance of outside sources. "Too much of a good thing is a bad thing," definitely applies to research writing. If you rely too heavily on outside sources (especially without reflecting on the content), the reader will suspect that you have no original ideas of your own. They may not even trust your final conclusions. In contrast, a lack of substantial evidence may lead the reader to believe that you have poor reasons for your claims. Above all, the supporting evidence must be relevant, having some logical connection or significance to the subject at hand.

To determine the relevance of supporting details, note the following items:

1) Examine the substance. Is the content complete and valuable, as opposed to being shallow and one-sided?

2) Identify the intended audience. Does the writer target a specific audience? Or is the subject too general as to be impractical and unrealistic?

3) Assess the author's background. Is the author credible because of his expertise and objectivity toward the subject?

4) Consider the timeliness of the article. Does this information apply to the present situation? For example, an article on computer technology from 30 years ago will not be as credible as an article written on the same subject just 30 days ago.

The more effort you put into finding accurate, reliable, and relevant sources, the more ideas you will find popping into your mind. This makes writing so much easier. For specific tips on finding the best research material, specifically on the internet, check out the PALBEG acronym in the next chapter.

5) Documentation. Whenever you use another's ideas, whether directly quoting that source or even paraphrasing their idea, you must give credit by referring to the source. Failure to give this credit is plagiarism, the claim that someone else's efforts in thought or writing are your own. In the academic world, this is equivalent to stealing. In the past, students have received no credit, have been suspended, or have even been expelled after plagiarizing. Much more importantly, plagiarism doesn't honor God.

One of the most common formats for giving such credit to sources is by following the guidelines of the Modern Language Association, known as the MLA style. Basically, the MLA style features two steps: the in-text citation, known as the parenthetical reference, and the works cited page. The in-text citation directly follows a borrowed idea with the author's last name and the appropriate page number in parentheses, for example, (MacDonald 392). There is no need to include the word "page," the letter "p," or a comma after the name. For guidelines on other in-text citations, such as multiple authors, anonymous works, internet sources, poetry, interviews, and more, check out some of the resources suggested at the end of this book.

The works cited page, attached as the last page of your paper, includes only the sources referred to in your paper. The most basic works cited entry for a book with one author includes the author's name, the title of the book, the place of publication, the publisher, and the year in which it was published. For example, *Passion and Purity* by Elisabeth Elliot would be written as follows: Elliot, Elisabeth. *Passion and Purity*. Grand Rapids, MI: Fleming H. Revell, 1984. For variations of other works cited entries, refer again to the list of Recommended Reading.

No matter what type of entry you use, there are some basic rules for the works cited page. You'll want to become familiar with these rules as you give credit to your sources:

○ Start each entry with the author's name, but place the last name first, followed by a comma and the first name. There is no need to include special titles, such as "Dr.," unless there is a suffix as part of the name, like "Jr."

○ Alphabetize each entry by the first letter of the last name, regardless of where the source appears in your paper.

○ Do not indent the first line of each entry; however, indent the second and any following lines of a single entry by five spaces.

○ Follow each segment of an entry with a period and one space.

○ As usual, capitalize all words in a title of a book, leaving articles, coordinating conjunctions, and prepositions uncapitalized, unless they begin or end the title.

○ Italicize or underline titles of books, journals, newspapers, etc.

○ Abbreviate all months except May, June, and July when you cite a magazine, newspaper, or journal entry.

- Shorten publisher names by excluding articles or business abbreviations and by abbreviating a university press to UP or U of (name) P.
- Double-space everything on the works cited page. This includes entries with more than one line, the space between entries, and the space between the title of the page ("Works Cited") and the first entry.

Depending on your region, college, or discipline of study, you may be required to learn and use a different format in research writing. Such examples of format include the American Psychological Association (APA), the Chicago Style, or the Council of Biology Editors (CBE). Always check your instructor's requirements before writing. Whichever style you use, remain true to a single style throughout the paper. Do not mix elements of different styles. For example, when writing with the MLA style, indent each paragraph by five spaces or hit the tab key once to indent. Do not use block style paragraphs.

6. Writing Style. Every time you pick up a pen, you reveal a unique writing style. Although style is subtle, it leaves a mark, much like a fingerprint. Style reveals who you are and what you think through your clarity, sincerity, and passion for the subject. However, no magical wand appears to bestow purposeful, captivating, and powerful words. Instead, practice develops your skill. The tone and formality, though, will depend on your intended audience and your purpose. The following strategies offer specific tips on how to develop your writing style.

- **Avoid First Person** – In college, your writing style and tone will be mostly formal. This approach demands that you avoid use of the first person perspective. In the concise book, *The Elements of Style*, the authors write, "Place yourself in the background. Write in a way that draws attention to the sense and substance of the writing, rather than the mood and temper of the author."[34] Structure your arguments around a solid framework of supporting points. If you truly desire to move your audience, the content of your words should be clearly organized and explained.
- **Be Original** – Begin every paragraph with your point – never a quote. (The exception here could be a quote in the introduction to capture the reader's attention.) Supporting evidence should be the strength behind your thoughts.
- **Write Naturally** – Avoid fluffy adjectives and lengthy descriptions. Such writing clouds your primary concern of capturing and maintaining your readers' attention. Also, don't overemphasize your ideas. If your supporting points do not adequately support your opinion, you'll need to revise your writing for clarity. Appealing to emotions through charged words does nothing to add credibility. In fact, most readers will dismiss your ideas as biased. As you write naturally, maintain balance. Avoid a conversational style with

slang. On the other hand, don't overcomplicate the issue. Write as clearly as your topic allows and include definitions to explain difficult terms. Use the proper terms recognized by experts on the subject.

- **Bring Ideas to Life** – Favor active over passive, state-of-being verbs. Include specific details, examples, images, metaphors, and similes to fight against vague and muddy explanations. To offset a lack of clarity, cut questionable qualifiers, like *sort of*, *rather*, and *very*. Because every word is important, avoid filler words, like *stuff*. While your opinion about the subject should be evident, a phrase like "in my opinion" or "I believe" is unnecessary. Research writing provides an opportunity to expose information or persuade your readers, making these phrases wordy and unnecessary. When you have properly cited outside sources, your ideas will be apparent to the reader.

- **Vary the Sentence Structure** – Because overly long sentences can confuse readers, you may need to divide your ideas into two or three shorter sentences. Use variety. Be brief and clear. A steady barrage of short, choppy sentences, however, appears childlike and overly simplistic. It takes a little practice to develop the skill to determine how, when, and where you will condense or connect thoughts.

- **Build Upon Ideas** – Work from the simplest points to the most complex. Start with the foundation, or what is known, gradually developing concepts that are more difficult. Even in a single sentence structure, end with the newest terms or most important information. This simple technique leaves an impression by emphasizing the idea.

- **Watch Mechanics** – Don't create your own exceptions to standard rules of English grammar, mechanics, and spelling. You are not e. e. cummings, the eccentric poet of the 1900s who introduced his own changes to traditional forms of structure and technique. In your papers, most instructors will not view the failure to capitalize under the positive lens of "creativity."

STRATEGIES FOR SMOOTH RESEARCH

The real key to writing a research paper is to break the big project into smaller, bite-size pieces. If you wait until the night before the final paper is due, your writing won't be very effective. Procrastination defeats the whole purpose of learning more about the topic because you're forced to cram all the ideas into a short and often scattered assembly of information. This does not lead to meaningful research or an improvement in writing skills; instead, it leads to stress, frustration, and exhaustion. Plan ahead. Don't be like the sophomore who said, "The only 'A' paper I've ever written was when I thought the due date was a week earlier than it was. It was amazing how many times

I 'tweaked' it during that extra week."[35] Shortly, you will view the Research Checklist to use as a model on your next research paper. Before you adapt this model to suit your instructor's requirements, examine the following strategies for smooth research. To write your papers more effectively, you should approach these strategies in order.

1) Brainstorm to Gather Ideas. Many students mistakenly construct an outline before they've done any research, expecting that any evidence they gather will neatly fit their plans. They think that because the outline serves as a skeleton form of the paper, they can then begin to research. However, this doesn't leave an opportunity for the research to actually show them something new – something more than their preconceived ideas about the topic. The whole point of research is to explore an issue in depth.

Obviously, you can't write a paper on an unfamiliar topic until you have found out what is important to know about that subject. In the same sense, you can't create an outline until you have discovered the essential evidence supporting your topic. Therefore, it's important to do some preliminary groundwork – a brainstorming or idea-gathering phase – so that you will know which points to emphasize and which points to downplay throughout the paper. Only after you've gathered all the ideas for your paper can you begin to orchestrate an outline. A "brainstorm web" or mind-map can be useful to gather ideas.

2) Find Material. The best strategy for a smooth project lies in the actual research-gathering phase. Although I've already discussed the element of supporting evidence, I can't emphasize enough the importance of finding accurate and relevant sources from reliable experts in the field. In a later chapter, we'll focus on determining the reliability of a source. For now, remember that gathering relevant evidence early is crucial whenever you're writing a research paper.

3) Plan Your Approach. Once you've gathered as much relevant information as possible, construct an outline, complete with Roman numerals, supporting points, and examples. As you design the outline, be sure to develop and explain the supporting evidence under your own ideas. When you actually sit down to write the paper, you can then let your own thoughts flow, connecting points with smooth transitions between paragraphs. In short, your ideas will make more sense because you'll have an outline to follow.

4) Write. When you actually do begin writing the paper, keep the following tips in mind:

○ Cover your points with solid reasons and supporting evidence.

○ Carefully choose your sources.

○ Use balance in using direct quotations.

- Stick to standard rules of sentence structure, grammar, and mechanics.
- Vary the sentence length and structure to add variety.
- Do not habitually start a paragraph with a quote or someone else's idea. After each quote, give your personal response.
- Ask yourself questions about your evidence: How does this add to or support my point? What new perspective or insight does this information give? Does this point support or contradict my other findings? In what ways?

Fill out your ideas by *discussing* the material you found. This is the proper way to conduct research, to build upon your own understanding, and to inform or persuade an audience.

5) Revise. Make corrections and ask a parent, teacher, tutor, or knowledgeable friend for feedback regarding both mechanics and content. Keep in mind that most colleges or universities provide a free writing center to help you polish a paper. The catch is that you cannot just drop off the paper and pick it up, laced with red corrections. You actually must sit down with a trained tutor and learn how to make the improvements.

6) Rewrite. The writing process should build toward a polished, final copy. Once you have written a couple of drafts, comb through and correct any final mistakes. Because your writing reflects the amount of thought and energy you have invested, your paper should reflect a confident and well-informed author.

This whole process is more manageable by simply planning ahead. Your professor will not question you every time you step foot in the classroom regarding the progress of your paper. Instead, you must pace yourself as though you are running a race. Set personal goals so that the final project does not remain an ever-present but unchallenged monster. The following provides a sample schedule of how to pace yourself in order to reach the finish line with little to no stress:

PERSONAL RESEARCH PAPER CHECKLIST

Breakdown of activities: **Week due**

_____ Choose your topic.   1

_____ Create a "brainstorm web" or mind-map on your topic.   1

_____ Develop your preliminary thesis statement.   1

_____ Find at least 5 relevant, reliable sources on the topic.   2

_____ Schedule an interview or design a survey.   2

_____ Make notecards from your sources by gathering supporting
         evidence, details, facts, and other data.   2-3

_____ Create bibliography cards.   3

_____ Complete interviews and surveys.   3

_____ Draft a thorough, logical outline of the paper.   4

_____ Begin writing, and create the first draft.   4

_____ Revise the initial draft. Ask a peer to read and make suggestions.   5

_____ Revise and complete the final draft.   5

_____ Prepared to present research, if required.   5

Warnings From a Whale
Your Guide to the Internet

CHAPTER 7

I once heard an interesting quote from Herman Melville, author of *Moby Dick*.

> *Isn't it curious that a huge whale can see the world through such a small eye, and hear the thunder with an ear smaller than a rabbit's? But if his eyes were as big as the greatest telescope and his ears as large as the doors of cathedrals, would that make him any longer of sight, or sharper of hearing?*

The ocean of interconnected ideas we call the internet is amazing. As we begin to research, though, we may wonder if bigger ears and eyes would help us take in more information. Of course, we know that outward, physical changes would do little to change how we gather and save those facts. In an age of information overload, I want the tools to distinguish the junk from the gems. This has never been more important than in the internet world, where anything goes. Sometimes it's easy to sift out the shallow evidence, faulty logic, and bad advice; sometimes it's hard.

We don't need bigger ears or eyes to gather this information – or even a larger memory to hold all the facts. Instead, we need tools to sift through this material.

A balanced approach to the internet helps determine the most worthwhile and useful sources. Although a few critics want to turn off the computer and return to the library, we must be realistic. The internet isn't going away; in fact, the information pool is constantly growing. As critical thinkers, we can adapt to the changes.

First, however, we need to consider its strengths and weaknesses. The following chart reveals both sides:

Advantages of Internet Research	Disadvantages of Internet Research
○ A variety of sources.	○ An excess of information and advertisements.
○ Nearly instantaneous results.	○ Time-consuming to sift through.
○ Short, pointed, condensed articles.	○ Prepackaged, diluted, often shallow articles with insubstantial evidence.
○ Good search techniques can pinpoint specific information.	○ Unrelated sources compiled by "spiders" or "worms" because of a single word recognition.
○ Access to academic journals, primary sources, eyewitnesses, or other experts on the subject.	○ Untrustworthy sources due to difficulty in checking background or facts.
○ Prompt reports of current events, weather announcements, and business information.	○ Time-locked: it does not fully cover information before the early 1990s.
○ Recent, possibly unpublished articles still unavailable at the library.	○ Outdated information on scientific research, medicine, and technology because these fields constantly change.
○ Option to communicate with authors, editors, webmasters, or others via e-mail, instead of through the mail.	○ Often regurgitated or repetitious

WATCH OUT!

Students today know a lot about technology – sometimes even more than their instructors. However, an advanced knowledge of "surfing" skills does not automatically mean you'll always choose the best sources. Adding to Melville's point on the whale, we find several warnings to the internet.

1) Don't be a ground feeder. College-level research depends on relevant, unbiased, and reliable sources. Anything less is junk. Unfortunately, it's easy to enter a search and find a host of both relevant sites and unrelated ones. One professor compared this problem "to the scholarly equivalent of 'roadkill' on the information superhighway because the student's sources contained inaccurate, incomplete, or misleading information."[36]

In other words, there's a big difference between collecting facts and thinking critically. "Quantity is the stuff of mediocrity: what distinguishes people of great talent and genius is the depth, detail, quality, and subtlety of their work."[37] As we gather information, we must *do* something with those facts and ideas. How do we respond to what we read and hear?

2) Don't be a parasite. Sometimes students rely on others' ideas instead of thinking for themselves. If we don't evaluate sites, the computer can become just as mind-numbing as the TV, at times. Like one professor said, "The biggest difference between (the computer and the television) should not be how close we're allowed to sit to the screen, but how much we are able to communicate with what is behind the images we see."[38] We don't need to shy away from using search engines or databases simply because there's a lot of information. Just as we need to learn to use the library's shelving system, we also need to learn how to track the best sources on the internet. The better we understand and develop the skills to test that information, the easier our own research will become.

3) Don't get bogged down. The internet is not regulated by standards or guidelines. On one hand, we have access to academic resources, journals, databases, research material, facts, visual aids, and other helpful information. However, the internet is also used to create and post unreliable evidence, incomplete facts, one-sided perspectives, and sites with prejudice and hatred. Unfortunately, some even benefit from scams, jokes, and other attempts to trick simple-minded and unsuspecting people.

> *The strength of the internet is also its problem: it has no gatekeepers. It's like a publishing house without editors or a library without librarians. Consequently, you have access to more than the publishers or librarians provide, but you bear the risk of not knowing what parts of it are worth reading, can be trusted, have been checked for errors, and so on.*[39]

Ignorance can be dangerous, so be aware of time-wasters and gimmicks as you search for meaningful information.

4) Don't swallow everything. Many sites offer a diluted mix of information and ideas. We often expect a neatly packaged, easy-to-absorb idea much like a can of condensed soup. Similarly, many internet sources offer a quick, shortened version of an idea. Professor David Rothenberg calls this the "hunt and peck method": a piecemeal gathering of ideas aided by the option to cut and paste. "A paper consisting of summaries of summaries is bound to be fragmented and superficial, and to demonstrate more of a random montage than an ability to sustain an argument."[40] True research demands diligence, dedication, and effort to see an idea through to its end. That takes time and effort to find great sources and to process our own ideas.

5) Don't ride the current. Many students think that whatever is most recent must be most accurate. Keep in mind, though, that "the last one to speak is not necessarily the one who holds truth."[41] Unfortunately, however, the last words we hear (or read) often stick with us the longest. We can be influenced by inaccurate evidence, but only if we leave that evidence unchallenged. We need to filter out unreliable sources.

DETERMINE THE RELIABILITY OF A SOURCE

To determine the reliability of a source effectively, we need to know what questions to ask. The acronym PALBEG offers an organized approach to ask questions before choosing sources for your research. Don't be overwhelmed by these questions; they're just offered as a resource in evaluating internet sites and articles.[42]

PALBEG

Category	What to ask as you read
Purpose	○ Why did the author write this article? To persuade, inform, entertain, refute, contrast, or record personal observations?
	○ Who is the intended audience?
	○ What is the underlying thesis or premise of the article?
	○ What is the author's point of view? (Pro, con, or neutral?)
	○ What conclusions, solutions, or implications does the author reach?
	○ Does the type of article shape or limit the information?
Authority	○ What are the author's qualifications to write this article?
	○ Is the author an expert, or does he quote experts?
	○ Was the author a witness or participant?
	○ Is the publication reliable and reputable?
	○ Do you have full publication data?
	○ Is the information in the article current?
	○ Is the article intended to be factual or editorial?
Logic	○ Can you identify any fallacies in logic?
	○ What points has the author selected and/or omitted? Why?
	○ How has the author organized the information?
	○ Is the reasoning logical and valid?
	○ What, if any, irrelevant material or arguments are presented?
Bias	○ Is the author subjective (biased) or objective (impartial)?
	○ What, if any, are the author's affiliations?
	○ Do historical reasons affect the objectivity of the author or his sources?
	○ What other points of view may exist but have not been discussed?
	○ What, if any, emotionally loaded language does the author use? Why? Give specific examples.
	○ Do the author's ideas and conclusions relate to your own experiences?
	○ Does the author's conclusion mesh with any previous reading, listening, or viewing you have done on this topic?

Evidence	○ Are the statements facts, opinion, or a combination of both?
	○ Has the author provided necessary background material on the topic?
	○ If the answer to the above is no, would the information be difficult to find on your own?
	○ Does the author's argument pass the following RET test:
	1) Is the evidence the RIGHT kind of evidence?
	2) Is ENOUGH evidence used?
	3) Is the evidence TRUE?
Gain	○ What does the author have to gain from the article? Consider power, money, influence, reputation, promotion, or personal meaning.
	○ What other factors may have influenced the author's writing?

EXPLORE YOUR RESOURCES

From these warnings, we might wonder how to get the most from PAL-BEG. Using the following approaches, we can find the best techniques for the most accurate research.

1) The Library – Start strong. Many sources recommend checking out your local library, especially if you consider the internet's disadvantage of being time-locked. Sometimes this can provide solid, substantial material faster than the time spent in browsing online. Through the library's catalog system, you can find reference books, encyclopedias, bibliographic indexes, academic journals, critical works, and much more. You can also speak with real people, librarians, that will help you through the research process. Some librarians even specialize in certain sections and can easily point out books that cover a topic in depth.

2) Databases. Beyond the physical library, databases, hosted online by most libraries, work much like a search engine. While Google or Yahoo may list thousands of unrelated sites on any given topic, databases offer a list of mostly reliable sources of substance. These sources have been filtered by a web librarian or other webmaster before being entered in the system. Examples of these databases include *GaleNet*, *EBSCO Host*, *InfoTrac*, *First Search*, *Pro-Quest Image*, *and Expanding lexis/nexis*. Specialized databases focus on more specific topics, such the *New York Times Index*, *Business Source Premier*, *ERICH*, *Literature Resource Center*, and *Earthscape*, to name a few. Your library's home page should provide links to begin searching through databases. Usually, you'll need to enter your library card number and PIN to begin a topic search on related material.

However, the articles on a database come in two forms: through bibliographic indexes or abstracts and in complete articles. An abstract offers a brief summary of the article with information on the author's background and reference locations to find the full article. Unfortunately, some students rely on abstracts as their source, instead of reading the actual article. This is like reading the back of a book without ever lifting the cover.

Relying on abstracts can hardly be called research. Only use an abstract to choose meaningful, relevant articles; then read the full text article to get an in-depth understanding of the subject. Students who fail to do so offer a cheapened version of thoughtfully developed ideas. As one professor writes of her students, "That is like bringing me a picture from a Denny's menu rather than the bacon cheddar burger and french fries I requested. In order to include a resource in your project, you must track down the actual article."[43] You can quickly limit your search by clicking on the full-text icon, if available. This will narrow the search results to those articles that are ready to print or save. Be sure to keep a record of the article by e-mailing a copy to yourself, saving through the copy-and-paste option (with the author's full background and publishing information), or by using the bookmark or "favorites" option. Before you print, be sure to click on the printer-friendly version, then click to find any related articles.

Finally, after exploring other databases, check out WorldCat. This database carefully filters relevant sources. Your search can be limited to internet sites only, offering you a highly selective approach to the World Wide Web.[44]

3) Now the Net. Once you have explored your database options, the internet can be used to find primary sources, online publications, academic journals, discussion groups, and helpful links. However, "Let the buyer beware," is a good motto to follow. "In the computer age, let the *researcher* beware... a good rule for critical thinkers: avoid anything you can't identify or verify."[45] Be suspicious of sites that do not allow you to identify the author or to verify and confirm its sources of information.

SEARCH ENGINE STRATEGIES

It's a lot easier to wade through a big search engine, like Google or Yahoo, when you have a plan and know some basic strategies. Before plunging into your usual search engine, use the following simple techniques to enhance your search. While some strategies may be basic, others may offer a fresh approach toward research.

1. If you know a specific website, use its URL, or uniform reference locator, to find the site.

2. With a keyword search, use the correct language or terms recognized by professionals in that particular field. When in doubt as to appropriate terms, check with the Library of Congress classification system at <http://www.loc.gov/>.

For example, replace the word "culture" with "social condition" or, more specifically, "division of labor."

3. Use an advanced search tool, usually found as a link on the search engine's home page.

4. Simplify a search with a whole phrase using parentheses or quotation marks around the words you would like in certain order. Use this technique with names – like "George Washington" – to eliminate unrelated articles on other topics like the children's author, Jean Craighead George, or the latest convention in Washington, D.C.

5. The Boolean system narrows your search when you add qualifiers like AND, OR, and NOT between keywords or phrases. For example, if you are researching a specific bird in a specific country of South America, enter "Toucan AND Panama NOT sight-seeing tour." This greatly reduces non-relevant sites from bogging down your search.

6. Use other qualifiers to narrow your search by requiring information with a plus sign or by excluding sites with a minus sign.

7. To search for related terms on your topic, use the "proximity" option by entering NEAR or ADJ (for adjacent). Otherwise, truncate a term to its shortest version; then use an asterisk or a question mark at the end. This technique is commonly referred to as the wildcard character.

8. Interact with the sites if possible. Jump into discussion groups or contact the webmaster, the person responsible for the site's contents, to ask questions or make relevant comments. These sources may offer suggestions or recommend excellent sources for your own projects.

9. Even when you find a solid article, remember that no single source on the internet will completely cover your topic. Therefore, it's important to look for basic categories (who, what, when, where, why, how, and to what extent) as you learn about your subject. Confirm the initial information by gathering additional articles to confirm and verify the information.

10. In addition to the PALBEG technique for choosing reliable internet articles, ask questions to evaluate websites:

- How effectively does this site cover the subject?
- Is the information original and unique in some way, but well-supported?
- How does it compare to other sites on this topic?
- How recently has the site been updated or maintained?

○ Are links, illustrations, audio, or video supplements easily accessible and relevant?

○ If there are any reviews about the site, do they provide balanced feedback?

○ Consider the context, along with the author's style and tone. Is the information ironic, satiric, idealistic, or deceptive?

A FINAL THOUGHT FROM THE WHALE

Only after students have honed their minds should we encourage them to tear through the vast haystack of garbage (read: the Web) to find the elusive needle of excellence; otherwise, they simply wallow in the trash.[46]

Now you're prepared to tackle the internet's ocean with useful tools to filter out a lot of useless information. The key to actually using these skills is practice. If you've only skimmed through the points in this chapter without thinking how you can best use them on your next project, you'll have missed some valuable, time-saving techniques. Use the technology we have to make your research worthwhile.

Of course, it takes more than just technology to write great papers. As Professor Rothenberg writes,

I wish that my university's computer system would crash for a day, so that I could encourage my students to go outside, sit under a tree, and read a really good book – from start to finish. I'd like them to sit and ponder what it means to live in a world where some things get easier and easier so rapidly that we can hardly keep track of how easy they're getting, while other tasks remain as hard as ever – such as doing research and writing a good paper that teaches the writer something in the process. Knowledge does not emerge in a vacuum, but we do need silence and space for sustained thought.[47]

Although Rothenberg isn't asking his students to ignore technology, he makes a good point. As we constantly adjust to what's going on around us, we need to process information thoughtfully. Such thinking requires time. As Melville said, we don't need bigger eyes and ears to understand information better. We just need to use the minds God has given us and become highly selective about the sources upon which we base our ideas and beliefs.

Character at College

CHAPTER 8

The bleachers filled as freshmen crowded into the gym. During the first week of college, we met often for orientation to the campus. At any moment, Dean John Talemy would be giving the welcome and announcements. While we waited, the hum in the bleachers gradually increased. I looked over as a girl with short brown hair waved wildly to a group of friends across the gym. To my left, a group of guys formed a huddle, but they suddenly broke out in laughter. Meanwhile, the dean had reached the front and now rested his arms on the podium. He waited a bit, finally tapping on the microphone to get our full attention.

"I'm glad to see your enthusiasm," he said with a smile. "But we need to get started. With great pleasure, I would like to introduce our guest speaker – my long-time friend, Professor Leland Ryken. He's just starting his 38th year of teaching at Wheaton College. He's also authored several books, including *Windows to the World and Realms of Gold*. From his years of working with students, he definitely understands the college experience. I've asked him to speak on what I consider to be an incredibly important aspect of college – the Christian student's calling. Please welcome with me Professor Leland Ryken."

As we clapped, we watched Professor Ryken approach the microphone.

Thank you for that, Dr. Talemy. I always look forward to an opportunity to speak with freshmen. Today, let me begin with a note that I found on the floor of my office one morning. It was from a student who had been absent from my Milton class during the preceding three weeks. It read,

Dr. Ryken,

I do not know where to begin, except I am preparing for the next test. I tried reading late into three successive evenings and found myself moving in and out of consciousness...I fell behind early after the first exam. This year I am heavily involved in the community. I am trying to wean myself from college life, but college is just a transition period. This term I have four reading courses, 20-30 hours in a ministry, a job, meetings almost every night, and two speaking engagements a week...

As you hear this, what do you think is the problem? It is not, on the surface, a deficient work ethic. Or is it? A healthy work ethic sets limits on work. This person is a workaholic. But at the root, the problem is a poor view of the student's calling or vocation. To be specific, college students are in a time of <u>preparation</u>, and that is their vocation until they graduate.

A Christian student's calling is the same as it is for a Christian in any vocation. Its focus is the individual's relationship to God. Loving and serving God should be the foundation for everything else that you do at college. It is a requirement, not an elective.

In the noblest of all educational writings, John Milton's <u>Of Education</u>, Milton gave this definition of Christian education: 'The end then of learning is to repair the ruins of our first parents (Adam and Eve) by regaining to know God aright, and out of that knowledge to love Him, to imitate Him, to be like Him.' Contrary to trends in our own century, Milton here defines education in terms of its end or goal rather than its means and techniques. What education should do, according to Milton, is produce Christian growth of mind, emotions, imagination, and soul. Milton is much less interested in how much you know than in the kind of person you are becoming during your college years. Of course, if you do not know much and do not value knowledge, that is an important part of whom you are in the process of becoming...

Hopefully, the goal of your education at college is to continue becoming more like Christ. You might graduate with a high GPA. You might also get into the graduate school of your choice. But if you haven't grown in Christian virtue and remained in some measure a whole person during your years here, you'll have missed the mark.

For a Christian, all of life is God's. It isn't divided into sacred and secular. What goes on in chapel or small groups is not inherently more important than what goes on in the classroom or library or dorm room. We have no basis for viewing some academic courses as sacred and others as secular. Nor are some academic majors holier than others. God calls Christians to make His will prevail in every area of life. Let me summarize. An education is adequate only if it educates the whole person for all of life.[48]

As I look back at the first week of orientation, I understand now why Dr. Ryken chose this topic on the Christian student's calling. So many times during college, I felt like I was losing a battle while treading water. I lost sight of priorities and got bogged down in the busy-ness of it all. I was missing the point of college – to glorify God in the details of my present circumstances as I prepared for His plans for my future.

Dr. Ryken's address is a challenge to the mindset of many students today. Excellent students stand out simply because of their humble, teachable spirits, personal motivation and effort, and a love of learning for its own sake. This mindset helps them enjoy the *process* of learning, not just the end result of a degree after four years.

To get the most from your own experience, get to know your instructors. Dr. David Dunn, a professor at Northwestern College in Minnesota, writes,

> Take advantage of the access that you have to your professors. Especially at small private schools, they really want to talk with their students. Ask questions! Today it seems that students are more comfortable with confusion. Get your questions answered now. The best time to ask a question is in class when the question arises.[49]

Of course, questions need to be appropriate and timely. Usually, instructors are willing to help, if you don't wait until the last minute. In fact, most professors post office hours to discuss students' questions or concerns. Dr. Boyd Seevers adds,

> I appreciate interaction with students. I enjoy getting to know them and interacting with them about what we cover in class as well as just talking about life. I appreciate the students who take the time and make the effort to make contact outside of class as well as in class.[50]

By respecting the student-teacher relationship and by cultivating the desire to learn for the sake of learning, your journey through college will be much smoother.

WHAT MAKES A GOOD STUDENT?

At college, expect variety. Even professors will have different teaching styles and philosophies about education. Some professors are highly professional, wearing suit-coats and ties, while others are more relaxed, sometimes sporting t-shirts and jeans. Some professors lecture for the entire hour; others follow a prepared PowerPoint presentation; and still others opt for more informal class discussion and small group interaction.

Regardless of the teaching style, prepare yourself to get the most from the classroom experience. Good students are not necessarily gifted; they do not possess superhuman skills beyond the capacity of the average student. However, there are specific characteristics or virtues of the students that stand out. By the standards of many professors, being a good student means being…

1) Teachable. College students pay big bucks for a degree, but good students recognize they have something to learn. This makes them humble and willing to accept advice, even when they didn't ask for it. Although it's a basic concept that professors are paid because they have something to teach, many students no longer value an instructor's authority on a subject. These students have somehow forgotten their role in the classroom.

Dr. Ryken elaborates on this virtue by writing,

I believe that the foremost virtue that you can display as a student is a teachable spirit. You are in a college precisely because you do not yet know all that is valuable to know. I believe that the highest praise I can write on a recommendation, apart from the earnestness of a person's Christian faith, is that the person has a teachable spirit. To be teachable means to be willing to learn from those – chiefly your professors – who have studied a subject thoroughly and have therefore earned the right to impart knowledge…[51]

It's tough to work with overly confident students, especially when they haven't really done their best work. For example, I once had a student who was angry about failing a persuasive research paper that she clearly plagiarized. I had evidence where material was cut and pasted from eight different internet sources, without a single word of credit to the authors. When we made an appointment to work outside of class and relearn the steps of citing sources, she never showed! This definitely sent a message on her willingness to learn.

2) Respectful. Good students value what instructors have to say. They carry a high opinion of a professor because of his *position of authority* on a subject – whether or not they agree with him. You may completely disagree with a professor's worldview and ethical position on issues, and you may find opportunities to discuss issues in class. At other times, you'll need to speak with instructors after class. Either way, you still need to approach them in Christ-like love and grace.

Even in less significant issues, like grades, Dr. Seevers writes,

I expect that students will disagree with me at times in matters such as interpretation of course material and in grading. I welcome their comments and input, though I find that comments are easier to deal with when made in a polite and respectful manner.[52]

Too many students badger instructors over what they consider to be an unjust grade. Little do these students realize, though, that their approach is wrong. Nothing is gained through disrespect – even if a professor made a mistake.

On a lighter note, respect is shown by the way a student carries himself in the classroom, but preparation starts well before class begins. Dr. Tanya Grosz writes, "Get to class on time. It's a waste of your money and disrespectful to your professor and classmates if you are late."[53] I've even heard of one professor at Connecticut College who locked the door after class started. If a student came late, the class would vote on whether or not to admit that student. At first, the class always voted "yes." But after a while, they got sick of the interruptions, and started voting "no."[54]

In addition to getting to class on time, you should stay awake and engaged. Pay attention, ask relevant questions, and take notes. Remember basic supplies like your book, completed homework, a notebook, and a pen. It distracts the professor and your classmates when you constantly have to borrow something.

One of the most obvious but overlooked measures of respect is to read the syllabus. Most professors hand out this course outline on the first day of class to give students an overview of what to expect. They often include specific requests – like turning off your cell phone and taking off your hat. Being aware of their wishes is one way to show respect.

3) Responsible. At the college level, you are responsible for your own education. If you miss a lecture, the professor will not chase you down with notes. That means that your education is on your shoulders. As Dr. Leanne Sponsel warns,

> *YOU are responsible for your college experiences - down to the paperwork. For example, if you lose an assignment or a class syllabus - YOU are responsible for replacing it. Ask to make copies from another student - DO NOT expect the professor to supply you with a second copy. Also, you are responsible to make appointments with your advisor; don't expect that she or he will call you.*[55]

With new responsibilities and pressures at college, it can be tough to persevere and see a challenge through to the end. However, "Students who are virtuous will always succeed in college." Dr. Clyde Billington continues,

> *Virtues such as reliability, self-control, self-discipline, a good attitude, and maturity are the keys to success in college, and in life itself. Ask any college professor, and she/he will tell you that the overwhelming reason why students fail is*

because they skip class and don't do assignments. I would estimate that failure to attend class accounts for 90% of college failures. College failure is very seldom caused by a lack of intelligence.[56]

It's a real temptation to skip class, especially one you don't enjoy, when your friends are skipping. While you're capable of making your own decisions at this point, you're also accountable for your actions. Sometimes you have to choose between what's fun at the present and what's a priority for your future. It's part of the territory of making decisions independently.

4) Self-Disciplined. Part of being a good student involves the dedication and effort to complete assignments well and on time. However, this requires the ability to do what is necessary without needing to be pushed and prodded by someone else. In fact, Dr. Douglas Huffman says, "The higher one goes in academic life, the more education is dependent upon the learner and not the teacher."[57] Many freshmen scramble at first because they've never had to create and keep a schedule on their own. It can also be tough to turn down friends who are going out for a movie or pizza because you have to study.

As Dr. Billington writes,

Some very good students in high school will fail in college because, when they lived at home, mom and dad supplied the needed virtues. But at college, these same students will fail because they lack their own self-discipline and have not internalized their parents' virtues.[58]

Self-discipline is personal. It's having self-control and knowing your limitations. But it's also training yourself to do things that you don't always enjoy, like studying for an exam or doing the research for a paper. In short, self-discipline is the ability to keep the things you can control in order, even when no one else gives their input.

5) Motivated. Good students are eager to learn. They view learning as a reason to study, a purpose in itself. This makes education a process, not just a means to an end. Like the self-disciplined student, the motivated student has enough interest to learn and stick with a subject, even when it gets hard. Unfortunately, for some, this is a personal drive that can't be borrowed from others.

Non-motivated students are bored with learning. Instead of evaluating information, they blindly accept ideas without thinking for themselves. Their apathy in the classroom is usually a failure to think, evaluate, and question incoming information. That's because learning can be tough. It takes effort to fight laziness and the appeal to accept everything mindlessly.

Dr. Ryken calls motivation the "spark," the intellectual curiosity to learn something new: "One of the best things that your college education can do for you is that you leave college being a student.[59] How is such a "spark" seen? Through self-motivation. Take the initiative to learn. Get to know your classmates, compare notes, and form study groups. Don't be so concerned about the number of words your professor requires on the next research paper. Instead, be much more concerned with what you'll say and how you'll say it. What will you take away from the assignment?

6) Prepared. Success is the offspring of planning wisely and applying effort. Good students know that it takes a lot of hard work and dedication to finish their work to the best of their abilities. But this doesn't happen overnight. Being an able student means being prepared. Good students are in a position to *do* something because they are mentally prepared.

Being prepared "requires a commitment to intellectual work, which, in turn, requires you to bypass some occasions of entertainment. God wants us to work hard in the things that matter to Him."[60]

As Dr. Tanya Grosz adds, "Don't expect A's right away. What earned you an A in high school may not earn an A at the college level. Don't be discouraged by this; just work harder."[61]

7) Balanced. Good students work to keep balance in their lives. This means saying "no" to some things so that they can say "yes" to others. This also gives them freedom to choose the best things, instead of letting people or events take over time that could have been used for studies, for example.

I recall my first week of classes. Table after table promoted programs, activities, and clubs to join. Each one sounded fun. It was a way to plug into campus right away. Being new, it also seemed like an easy way to make friends. But as I look back, I see how fast the time went. Some of the activities were a lot of fun – like the rock climbing group I joined, which met once a month. Other groups, like the volleyball team, took too much time with practice and travel. For me, a better option was the intramural volleyball team, which was a lot less stressful but still let me play during the week.

So what's the point? Balance is the key to a stress-free college experience. I've known students who burn out because their lives were out of balance. They didn't seem to ever have any time, and they were always running late.

In my own life, when I'm busy, it's hard to keep up with my devotions each day. When a Christian's relationship with the Lord isn't consistent, everything else in life is off-kilter. It's hard to make decisions clearly and harder still to work well with others.

A FINAL CONSIDERATION

The attitude and techniques through which you approach your studies make all the difference to your success or failure as a student. Of course, only you have control over how you, personally, view your education. Eventually, perhaps even without fully realizing it, you'll decide for yourself what you value in an education.

If you decide to attend a Christian college, take advantage of the time. A professor's wisdom often extends beyond the classroom into real life situations, and many are willing to talk with you outside of the classroom. As Professor Randy Nelson writes,

> *Most Christian professors see their job as a ministry. For that reason, they are interested in more than just the student's intellectual development. Students should seize the opportunity to seek out different professors as they attempt to discern God's call on their lives or discern God's will on different issues.*[62]

College is a time to learn and grow into a well-rounded person. The freedom to make personal choices is new and exciting, but balance is key. It's also important to fine-tune the other character traits of a good student: being teachable, respectful, responsible, self-disciplined, self-motivated, and prepared. These traits will get you far, not just as a student, but as a person for life.

Part 3 – Purpose

Worlds Apart

CHAPTER 9

College is very different from the comfort zone of wherever you called home. Here you'll meet people from all different walks of life with vastly different ideas. Each person carries a set of beliefs about how the world works. Even if a person can't define that view, it directly influences choices, actions, and relationships. This worldview reveals *who* a person is and *what* that person believes and values. But a worldview is not just based on words – claims of belief. It's revealed through actions, which often provide a better gauge of where the heart actually lies.

Take, for example, Lorenz Hart, the lyricist who composed songs with Richard Rodgers. Their Broadway breakthrough came in 1925, but in spite of their success, Hart wasn't satisfied. Heavy drinking followed, and he eventually split with Rodgers, who began working with Oscar Hammerstein. Together, Rodgers and Hammerstein gained popularity on such musicals as *The King and I*, *South Pacific*, and *The Sound of Music*. Hart, on the other hand, was growing more depressed. Shortly before his death in 1943, he posed the tragic question, "What have I lived for?"[63] The tragedy of Hart's question reveals the emptiness of his life. Like Hart, many people don't ask the real questions about life until they reach death.

The college campus is a breeding ground for ideas and conversations. That doesn't always mean you're going to run into people with real truth, though. Whether you go to a Christian college or a secular university, you're going to meet a lot of people – some with very different ideas about God, reality, right versus wrong, and life after death. As you talk with professors, classmates, and co-workers, is it enough just to agree to disagree? Or is there a higher standard – some Absolute Truth – that will measure us all?

In your own college experience, you'll be challenged to provide evidence for why you believe what you believe. That's the reality of putting your beliefs to action. While this can be scary at times, it's also exciting, especially on a secular campus where there are so many opportunities to speak the truth. As we begin this section on worldviews, I ask you to examine who you are and what you believe – before you ever step foot in a college classroom. Christians can make a difference, not just as moral people or conservatives, but as living witnesses of how Christ can change a life.

DEFINING A WORLDVIEW

A worldview makes up a person's ideas about life, but it doesn't end there. This is not the ability to spout off a religious code, even though many people can do this quite well. A worldview is also not just a product of one's surroundings or home life.

Instead, a worldview progresses and develops, sometimes subtly over time, sometimes dramatically in an instant. It evolves as we understand our beliefs better. This makes a worldview fluid.

However, it's important to remember that we're not always consistent in our actions and beliefs because we are imperfect creatures. While ideas within a worldview influence actions, our actions may not always mirror what we desire our beliefs to be. In spite of this, actions still reveal our hearts. A worldview's ultimate test reveals true character, even when no one is watching.

In his book, *Naming the Elephant*, James W. Sire defines this concept of a worldview as

> *A commitment, a fundamental orientation of the heart, that can be expressed as a story or in a set of presuppositions (assumptions which may be true, partially true, or entirely false) which we hold (consciously or subconsciously, consistently or inconsistently) about the basic constitution of reality, and that provides the foundation on which we live and move and have our being.*[64]

Of course, ten different people might each give you a different set of ideas about how the world works, but that does not change what is ultimately true. Furthermore, I can tell you what I believe as truth based on the Bible, but that alone will not make it real for you. As you read, I encourage you to seek these answers for yourself. Do not mindlessly accept everything you hear. This only leads to a false sense of security – false because it is based on another's beliefs about life. *You* must know why you believe what you believe.

WHY BOTHER?

According to a report from a UCLA dissertation by Dr. Gary Railsback, one out of every two to three students renounces their faith by the time they leave college.[65] Admittedly, a Christian may struggle with questions as he comes to understand what he truly believes. However, these struggles within the Christian faith can be fruitful because they expose a person to unknown weaknesses. By resolving these issues as they arise, a person is better equipped to "fight the good fight" and stand firm with conviction.

However, with so many young people renouncing their faith, I begin to wonder if they actually *owned* it for themselves. Like a parrot, a young person may repeat ideas of right and wrong and mouth the family's religious beliefs. Like a puppet, a young person may comply with and conform to his religious circles. However, if Christ has truly changed one's life, there is no coercion or faulty pretenses. A real Christian life of peace comes from knowing where one truly stands before God. Being raised in a Christian home and taught Christian values doesn't make someone a Christian. Beliefs aren't genetic. A Christian's worldview becomes alive when beliefs change actions. Thus, a worldview is only partially revealed by what we say. A worldview is better revealed by how we respond to people and situations.

We live in a day when basic values of right and wrong are questioned. As a result, there is a higher rate of liberalism among college freshman now than at any time since the Vietnam War. According to a survey of freshmen taken by the Cooperative Institutional Research Program,

- 57.9% think gay couples should have the legal right of marriage;
- 36.5% think marijuana should be legalized;
- 32.2% want to abolish capitol punishment;
- and 29.9% claim that they are liberals or "far left."[66]

Why is it that so many young people now hold these views? Could it be that they have leaped into the world (specifically the academic world) without the proper equipment?

As Christians, we have an opportunity to take a stand for what's right. All too often, however, Christians are poorly equipped for combat because they haven't taken the time to know Truth from God's Word. How can they defend what they have not studied? In short, they do not know where they stand or what they believe. The authors of *Honey for a Teen's Heart* write, "As teens put together their worldviews, they need to be able to verbalize what they believe not only so that they can share it with others, but also to see how their beliefs are shaping in their own lives."[67]

This vision is what Sire calls the "tools of analysis" when we reflect on our own beliefs, as well as the beliefs of others at school and in our culture.[68] We can examine our own beliefs and actions for the purpose of lining up under God's standards. As we think about other ideas, we begin to understand why some people respond as they do when we witness. Out of Christ-like love, we can become a voice for change in a country that tries to hide its Christian heritage. At school, we can stand up for Truth in the classroom as we challenge false assumptions.

A study in worldviews shows us the relationship between ideas and actions. To a degree, it's important to *be aware* of where others are coming from. Ultimately, however, there is an absolute standard of truth, God's Word, which should be our main focus. This Book helps us prepare for the future. According to I Peter 3:15, we study in preparation for responding to the hope that lies within. If we, as Christians, are to respond at all, we must know why we hold our beliefs. However, we need discernment to be "wise as serpents and harmless as doves" (Matthew 10:16). As we follow Christ's example of love, we can live with confidence.

A WORLD OF DIFFERENCES

What follows below is a brief explanation of today's common worldviews. While this topic can be complicated, I've tried not to generalize or oversimplify ideas. Although I recognize the fact that different forms do exist within each view, this is just a sketch of supporting principles.

While it's important to be aware of major differences in beliefs, it is not necessary to memorize every detail of these concepts. What is important is to *listen* to what people say before you respond. The goal here is simply to bring awareness to how very different some views are from one's own as you prepare to respond.

- **Deism** – Deists think of God as Creator, but they believe that he left the universe to figure things out for itself. One explanation uses an old, wind-up clock. Someone has wound up our world, but left it to run down on its own. The universe is an intricate but closed system in which humans may attempt to reason. "Closed" means there are no miracles to fix problems, and circumstances are based simply on cause and effect. Because humans are part of this system, they can't be held accountable for errors or problems. Deists, therefore, reason that God should be held responsible for the way things are because, although he has left the clockwork, he designed it. Alexander Pope, a poet of the eighteenth century, summed up such beliefs by writing, "Whatever is, is right."[69] Today, we see this view through books and movies that bring up God but show individuals solving problems alone as they determine right from wrong.

- **Naturalism** – The naturalist combines science and philosophy with romanticism. Reason replaces God, and matter alone exists. For example, check out the following quote:

  We are composed of the exact same atomic matter as the mightiest mountains on this planet and the brightest stars in this galaxy. Of course, this is also true for potatoes, snails, and meatloaf – perhaps that's why there's so much about life that doesn't make a great deal of sense."[70]

  In this view, man determines right from wrong and establishes values. History has no purpose in itself; instead, it is simply a domino effect of events in response to prior events. Society is the end-all because it creates a set of conditions to better humanity. Death is final because matter ceases to exist. One form of naturalism includes secular humanism, the overemphasis of the human being. Another example is the humanism of Karl Marx, or Marxism. Of course, Marx's dying words illustrate this view: "Go on, get out. Last words are for fools who haven't said enough!"[71]

- **Nihilism** – "Death is nothing, nor life either, for that matter. To die, to sleep, to pass into nothingness, what does it matter? Everything is an illusion."[72] Such a statement embodies the feeling of nihilism. In a word, this view is "nothingness." Under this view, there is no God. There is no right or wrong. Furthermore, there are no values, such as civilization, marriage, property, or justice, because these are only lies formed by society. Within this concept, there is only emptiness apart from self and the pursuit of happiness. Politically speaking, nihilism results in anarchy, or the attempt to overthrow any system of laws or social order. As one bumper sticker suggests, "Maybe the hokey-pokey is really what it's all about." Such emptiness sometimes leads to suicide because one's existence without hope brings utter meaninglessness.

- **Existentialism** – This concept focuses on man's existence in order to bring significance to a meaningless world. Existentialists believe that expectations of human nature are created by the culturally elite to control people. People do not possess virtues or values. Instead, the individual is merely a product of choices. In other words, people must live with the consequences of their choices, but they don't need to justify their decisions. To be good, one must be conscious of such choices, regardless of the outcome. In addition, because existentialists do not rely on the accuracy of history, they distrust written records. This greatly affects today's classroom. Specifically, a current trend discredits American historical events based on the belief that an elite group of "white men" created our history books to control American minds. Under the existentialist umbrella, however, live two quite different branches, one believing there is a God, the other denying his existence. A recent television series is one example of existentialism in that it portrayed God in disguises of various characters coming to offer advice as the young protagonist struggles with daily decisions.

- **Eastern Pantheism** – A Westerner struggles to understand even the concept of Eastern Pantheism, but here are the basics. Pantheism means that god is in all; god is in all of us as the One. Each human's soul makes up the Soul of what is cosmos, but some people are just more in touch with that essence than others. Those who are nearest to pure being are considered the Perfect Master or the Enlightened One. What is difficult for Westerners to grasp, however, is the impersonal nature of this view. The Oneness is abstract. If a person is to realize fully this essence, one's individuality must be surrendered to move beyond knowledge, good, and evil. Under this view, any given moment holds perfection. There are no right or wrong answers because each person's answer is acceptable. For example, on my first day of college, my English professor calmly walked to the front of the room and announced, "In this class, there are no right or wrong answers." I looked around at my classmates. What did she mean? Would everyone earn an 'A' regardless of what we turned in? For a Pantheist, harmony lies within each person who must focus energy on that center within oneself. Mind, body, and spirit interconnect. When a person dies, that individual no longer exists, but the larger Soul is preserved. Death does not change an individual's essence because that person can return as something else, through reincarnation, for example. Modes of reaching this Oneness during life include meditation, contemplation, and simplification. As one student said, "I am a human being, not a human *doing*."[73] Hinduism and Zen Buddhism are key religions within this worldview.

- **New Age** – The mystical New Age Movement combines elements of Eastern Pantheism, theism, and naturalism. This optimistic worldview attempts to bring hope for humanity through psychic phenomena and supernatural experiences. Personalities within this movement include channelers (or mediums to the spirit world), witch doctors, and faith healers. Familiar icons representing this movement include crystals, acupuncture, and drugs – anything that enables one to access both the physical world and the larger universe, or "Mind at Large." There is no fear of death when one is using such mediums. In the New Age Movement, the self is God. Humans can achieve cosmic consciousness and transcend space, time, and morality. The general idea is to be both at one with the universe and to perceive the universe as a whole in order to experience the self as the ultimate reality. In short, the New Age Movement is "a Western version of Eastern mysticism in which the metaphysical emphasis of the East is replaced by an emphasis on seeing, experiencing, or perceiving the unity of reality."[74] The *Star Wars* series illustrates how this concept denies any use of reason, as we saw through Luke's training by Obi-Wan: "Luke, trust your feelings. Use the Force, Luke. Let go. Trust me."[75] As David Quine writes, the irony of this picture, however, is that "those displaying the greatest rationality and thought were actually robots!"[76]

○ **Postmodernism** – The fatalistic and skeptical philosophy of postmodernism thrives in our society. In this thought system, God is dead. We are alone and adrift to use our sense of reason as we can. Since there is no ultimate truth, any one person's ideas hold as much validity as the next. Such relativism permeates our conversations with simple phrases like, "To each his own." Reality and truth only exist from what each person creates for himself. Thus, contradictory ideas exist, but debate is pointless because there are no absolutes. Many college classrooms have been silenced by such apathy. What is the point of discussion? To find one's truth, however, we have a growing storehouse of literature and videos with open endings – purposely open for interpretation. "The truth about reality is forever hidden from us. All we can do is tell stories."[77] To understand our silent world, we must use language to communicate and bring meaning. Every experience, much like existentialism, is based on personal interpretation. Stories in and of themselves are potentially powerful because they provide an opportunity to express truths about life. Postmodernism stems from and answers modernism, which used the arts to aid the human condition. This focuses on the individual's ability to reason. The writings of author Fredrick Nietzsche are examples of postmodernism.

FINDING ABSOLUTES

But wait, you may object. Haven't I left out a worldview? Yes. I've intentionally saved one by which all others pale. Actually, there is no comparison because real hope exists within this worldview. Humanity is not left to blindly wade through problems using social standards or human reason. There is beauty, not emptiness, in what God has created and established. We have access to a real and living God without using physically dangerous forms of mind alteration. In stark contrast to the Zen philosophy of life, there is so much more to reality than what our limited, finite minds can grasp. *Absolute Truth exists*, and *it stops all other interpretations of reality.*

In Christian theism, God is at the center. But who is this God?[78] In an effort to offer a concise but biblically accurate answer to that question, an assembly of church officials gathered in 1647. *The Westminster Catechism* resulted, otherwise known as *The Confession of Faith*. In this definition, God is a Spirit, infinite, eternal, and unchangeable, in His being, wisdom, power, holiness, justice, goodness, and truth.

Because God is a Spirit, He is not bound by anything. He is everywhere, but He is formless and intangible. God is infinite in that He is perfect – He cannot be added to, diminished, or divided. However, He is definite at the same time; that is how He hears all Christians' prayers at the same time throughout the world.

Another aspect of God's being is that He is eternal. There was nothing before Him; He created all things in eternity from one act of power. Although we experience events in time, God is outside of time. Thus, God is unchangeable in that He does not learn anything new, nor is He surprised by anything. To be so would be to limit His omniscience, or knowledge of all things.

In spite of tragic events that happen, God uses circumstances for His purposes and His perfect plan. As Romans 8:28 says, "All things work together for good." In short, His ways are perfect because He is perfect. God is also omnipotent, or all-powerful. His power doesn't run low when He's working in another person's life. In addition, God is perfectly holy in his purity and hatred of sin, and He reveals His absolute standards for what is right and wrong through His justice. However, God also reveals His goodness through His love, mercy, and grace to us. We can trust Him because of His faithfulness or inability to lie.[79]

Our utter amazement in learning about this God is that He makes Himself personal to us. God is the Creator, and we are the created. But man, while created in God's image, is fallen. This separates us from having a relationship with God. Fortunately, however, that's not the end of the story.

God has provided a way for us to know Him. That way is Jesus Christ, who himself proclaimed, "I am the Way, the Truth, and the Life; no man comes to the Father but by Me." (John 14:6) Here, we have absolutes. We are in desperate need of a Savior to aid us in our fallen state and to bring us to the one, true God (Colossians 1:15-23). With this knowledge and belief in Jesus Christ comes a sense of purpose and meaning in life. When we really embrace the idea that our purpose in life is to honor Christ in everything, we find true joy and peace. Since we were created in God's image, we can share in some of His attributes, like wisdom, justice, goodness, and creativity. But this doesn't make us little gods because we're still imperfect humans. Instead, we can become more like Him as He reveals Himself to us through the Bible and His created world. This understanding of who God is, then, directly influences our concepts of self and the world around us.

A WORLDVIEW EXPOSED

A Christian's focus in life should be to bring God glory in all things, and we can do this through such a study in worldviews. However, a worldview is not simply what we say is true. There's a difference between talking and actually living out one's beliefs. A worldview determines how we live, act, and respond to the world around us.

If we are to be effective witnesses of what Christ has done, we must know what we believe as truth and why we believe it to be true. We also need to actually live out the beliefs that we claim to possess in a Postmodern era. The "tools of analysis" help us reexamine personal beliefs and identify the worldviews of others in order to make a difference on our campuses and in our culture. As Christians, we can confront liberalism, tolerance, and moral relativism with absolute Truth.

This makes the Christian theist's worldview much more than a simple study in religion. As Sire writes, "To be a Christian theist is not just to have an intellectual worldview; it is to be personally committed to the infinite – personal Lord of the universe. And it leads to an examined life that is well worth living."[80] You may have been raised under a specific belief structure that influences the way you view the world. In fact, you may be quite moral with a strong set of ethics to support how you live. However, this only makes you a "good person" from the world's perspective. As C.S. Lewis writes, the Christian understands that,

> *Any good he does comes from the Christ-life inside him. He does not think God will love us because we are good, but that God will make us good because He loves us; just as the roof of a greenhouse does not attract the sun because it is bright, but becomes bright because the sun shines on it.*[81]

The Bible is a Christian's "sword" to cut through the emptiness of words. However, we must handle this tool with care, never using it to puff ourselves up with mere facts to show others that we are the keepers of all wisdom. Real Christian love is bold, honest, and forthright, but it is also gracious to others who do not know truth.

As Christians, we must live boldly, but that requires preparation and effort on our part. The goal of the next few chapters is exactly that – to equip you with courage as you face the unknown. This courage is found by facing uncertainties with the conviction and love of Christ.

And do not be conformed to this world, but be transformed by the renewing of your mind, that you may prove what is that good and acceptable and perfect will of God.

– Romans 12:2

CHAPTER

10

Break the Mold

In 1953, Sir Edmund Hillary and Tenzing Norgay reached the highest point on earth. Mount Everest towers more than 29,000 feet above sea level in the Himalayas of Nepal. Today, adventurers like John Shipton continue these expeditions up the North Ridge to experience the breathtaking view.[82] Aided by native Sherpas, he and his fellow hikers reach the peak by foot. Because the whole trip takes 71 days, immaculate attention to the details is crucial. Each climber must prepare both physically and mentally for the extreme adventure that lies ahead.

Seven years after the first trek up Mount Everest, Dr. Donald Walsh and a Swiss scientist, Jacques Piccard, broke a different record. The tiny vessel, *Trieste*, with one glass porthole eight inches thick, brought the two men to the deepest known point on the earth, the Challenger Deep in the Pacific Ocean's Marianas Trench. At 35,800 feet below sea level, it is extremely cold and dark. The pressure weighing down on the *Trieste* measured roughly 16,000 pounds per square inch. In spite of such extreme conditions, life still exists at this depth. A small, flat fish swam into Dr. Walsh's view. Later, after a safe return home, the two men received honors from President Eisenhower. To this day, Walsh and Piccard remain the only two humans to reach this depth.

Adventures like these inspire us, but they point to something far greater. Human potential is amazing only because God created us in His image. He's given us minds to think and to feel, to process information and to solve problems, to recall memories and to learn new skills. He's given us the intelligence to reason, imagine, design, and explore. We've climbed the Himalayas and descended the Challenger Deep, but God has also given us the capacity to probe other possibilities. With NASA, we're beyond walking on the moon as plans unfold for a livable space station. With modern medicine, computerized surgeries repair microscopic details of the human anatomy.

Technology and the intelligence to invent such wonders are gifts from God. Unfortunately, however, a lot of people don't recognize this relation to the Creator. The mind is a means to some personal end, such as fame or fortune. In *Ordering Your Private World*, Gordon MacDonald writes,

> *It's sad to see great thinking and artistic work accomplished by men and women who have no interest in uncovering a knowledge of the Creator. They think and innovate purely for self-aggrandizement or for the development of a human system that assumes it can get along without God.*[83]

As humans, we can appreciate the world around us. As Christians, we hold the capacity to use our resources and abilities with excellence for God's glory.

Sometimes, however, Christians get caught up in *how to* do this. Let's make it simple. In Romans 12:2, God renews the mind as we consistently study and think about His truths. This means that each thought affects the big picture of our lives. How is that possible? Thoughts form the base of a person's character, and this character is shown by how we live and act in the world. As Christians, we have a high calling because we have the capacity to think like Christ. Let me point out that it's only because of Christ that our minds are transformed in the first place. To renew our minds, it's important to study, ask questions, and know truth for ourselves.

Whenever we simply repeat ideas without processing those ideas for ourselves, we act like parrots. How can we talk about what we believe if we don't *study* and *think* about the truths of God's Word? Absorbing ideas without thought is like popping in a wad of previously chewed gum. All of the flavor and enjoyment has long since passed; instead, we are left with a lifeless form of rubber. We must think for ourselves to truly understand and own the ideas we value. Failure to do so is simply a reflection of what others value.

THE CHRISTIAN MIND

Christians have a unique responsibility with the mind. We can't simply accept everything we hear. A sponge-like absorption of opinions does little to establish truth in the mind. Christians, especially, should desire to understand and communicate *why* they believe what they *claim* to believe. The attitudes we possess toward developing the mind make all the difference in the choices we make and the way we act.

Knowing the truth requires effort on our part. Please, don't misunderstand me, though. Absolute truth and wisdom come from God who works through the Holy Spirit in the life of a Christian. In other words, we don't create truth; God reveals truth.

This means we have a responsibility to use and develop the minds we've been given. This balance is best described in the following statement by Dr. James Zaspel, author of a monthly newsletter, *The Connecting Link*:

> *God calls us to study, to learn, to grow in knowledge. Any shortcut to this is pure mysticism. There is never any premium placed on ignorance, but always on study, learning, meditating, and giving ourselves to the study of Scriptures. This is the means by which we grow, and this is the means by which we are equipped. It is illogical and irresponsible to think otherwise. Jesus said that the key to obeying the truth*

was knowing the truth. It is self-evident that our minds are to be receptors of truth, and not originators of truth. The sad thing is that Christians invest so little time and energy in learning what they claim to be the Word of God that it falls away by default. Hence, they become 'willfully ignorant' – an ignorance for which they will be held accountable.[84]

This brings up an interesting point: Some people are actually *afraid* to think for themselves because of what it requires. In fact, some Christians even create comfort zones based solely on rules and regulations. As MacDonald writes, these Christians,

Mistake the gathering of facts, doctrinal systems, and lists of rules for thinking. They are uneasy when dealing with open-ended questions. And they do not see the significance of wrestling with great ideas if they can't always come up with easily packaged answers.[85]

That's because it's sometimes easier to live by a man-made code of black and white. But Christians are called to a level of mental maturity, so that we aren't "carried about by every wind of doctrine" (Ephesians 4:14). We must use our minds to *hear* what others are saying and *ask questions*. We must use our minds to *evaluate* new ideas and *make decisions* for ourselves. We must use our minds to *weigh* the consequences of our actions as we strive to *bring honor to Christ*. While God ultimately changes the heart, we still play an active role in spiritual growth by our thoughts.

At the beginning of this chapter, we saw that God created us in His image. Now we see that Christians have an opportunity to challenge the world's value system with the truths of God's Word. Christians have the incredible honor of a call to know and to portray truth before the world. Yet how can we carry out this responsibility if we aren't diligent to study and use our minds well? Pastor John MacArthur emphasizes the importance of this kind of thinking:

If we want to distinguish intellectually between the good and the best, and make choices with integrity, we must think. It is imperative that we respond carefully with our minds and not impulsively according to emotion.[86]

WHAT IT MEANS TO THINK CRITICALLY

At first glance, the word "critical" seems negative, like focusing on someone's faults. However, this definition is a lot different when we look at it in relation to our thoughts. *Keys for College Studying* defines critical thinking as that which,

> *Goes beyond the basic recall of information but depends on the information recalled. It focuses on the **important, or critical, aspects** of the information. Critical thinking means asking questions. Critical thinking means that you **take in information, question it,** and **then use it** to create new ideas, solve problems, make decisions, construct arguments, make plans, and refine your view of the world.*[87]

The key here is to understand that critical thinking is a *process*. Check out the following chart to find out exactly what critical thinking involves.

What Critical Thinking Is	What Critical Thinking Is *Not*
○ Focused or intentional thoughts.	○ A-mused: the opposite of deep thinking.
○ A balanced approach to determining strengths and weaknesses.	○ Hasty, impulsive, or impetuous.
	○ Easily swayed by emotions or moods.
○ Includes observation, interpretation, explanation, and evaluation.	○ Incoherent or inarticulate.
○ Discretion or discernment.	○ Illogical or irrational.
○ Using reason or logic.	○ Indiscriminate or undiscerning: like a "sponge" ready to absorb all things.
○ Open-minded, in the sense of being willing to learn new things.	○ Unteachable; biased without reason.
	○ Foolish, simplistic, or gullible.
○ A process of reflection that includes becoming informed, asking questions, and applying information.	○ Immature in approaching challenging issues.
○ Creative: sees things in new ways.	○ Reflective: mirrors others' ideas.
○ A challenge in that it requires effort.	○ Takes the easier path.

Critical thinking isn't just a set of skills to learn. It's a habit formed by thinking through all the facts. Regardless of whether the initial reaction is to agree or disagree with that information, we must be willing to postpone our final judgment until after we're fully informed, hearing all sides of an issue. The result is an informed decision. As we work through ideas, we continue to learn and grow.

QUALITIES OF CRITICAL THINKING

Critical thinking requires time, effort, and practice. In our day, we rarely take time to think. We rush around to different activities, sometimes without even pausing to refresh our minds with God's truth. Missing this time, though, dulls our thinking, making us vulnerable and weak. Instead, we need to sharpen our ability to discern, the skill to distinguish things clearly. In his book, *How to Stay Christian in College*, J. Budziszewski writes that discernment "helps you choose the true and avoid the false, choose the good and avoid the evil. It's a mental sense of smell that helps you notice when 'something smells fishy.'"[88] This metaphor is a perfect picture of being aware and engaged to think critically.

There is a right attitude in critical thinking, though. It's important to be open – open in the sense of holding a humble and teachable spirit. This is not pridefully asserting one's views and humiliating others when they're wrong. On the other hand, critical thinking doesn't embrace all views when truth is being attacked. When discussing issues, a good approach includes the humility to admit when an argument is weak. (Of course, this may be a sign that you need to study a topic in more depth.) A right attitude also involves a willingness to change positions when you're proven wrong.

Remember, however, that critical thinking takes practice. Just as a weightlifter or runner trains, we need to give our minds practice to develop critical thinking. Yes, it can be challenging at times, but as MacDonald writes, we must put ourselves in a "growth mode." For the Christian, this requires discipline and training – to observe and appreciate God's creation and to pursue information and ideas as we serve others and bring glory to God.[89] Such a growth mode puts us in a mindset where we expect or *anticipate* our thoughts to be challenged. We are then ready to learn and grow because the foundation for critical thinking has been set. Some of the best strategies for developing this skill include the following:

- **Prepare –** Daily devotions are vital. As we spend time with the Lord, we learn to think His ways and "put off the old man." We are renewed and prepared for whatever comes into our path. The less disciplined we are in guarding the mind because it is "the wellspring of life," the more swiftly we will fall.
- **Listen –** At the most practical level, we simply must stop to listen to what's spoken or observe what's happening.

> *We grow through listening, aggressive listening: asking questions, watching intently what is happening around us, and taking note of the good or ill consequences that befall people as a result of their choice making.*[90]

If we are observant, we can learn through the failures and successes of others. However, this requires us to be actively engaged, mentally involved.

- **Think** – Since character hinges upon thought life, it's crucial to keep thoughts in check. As Pastor MacArthur writes,

    Out of our thoughts comes our conduct. Our true character is therefore defined by what we think, not how we appear to others, not what we say, and ultimately, not even how we behave. The truest test of character is the thought life. As a man thinks, so is he.[91]

Our thoughts influence our responses. "It is not what comes into a man that defiles him, but what comes out" (Matthew 15:17-18). If we are honest, we'll examine our first reaction when bad things happen. No matter the circumstances, this first response reveals a glimpse of who we truly are deep down.

- **Question** – One of the most effective ways to develop critical thinking is to ask questions. This skill requires tact to challenge unsupported ideas without insulting the speaker. In one analogy from Summit Ministries, asking questions is compared to a hammer. Although a hammer can be misused by someone inexperienced, "a question properly and strategically used can both drive a point home and pry open people's minds!"[92] This comparison is later followed by four deadly questions that get to the heart of any issue:

    1. What do you mean by that?
    2. How do you know that to be true?
    3. Where did you get your information?
    4. What if you are wrong?

Of course, these questions should be asked in good judgment and maturity, in a loving and careful manner. If we attack others just to prove they're wrong, we miss the point of challenging beliefs that oppose Christ.

- **Connect** – Get together with other, like-minded believers. As Hebrews 10:25 notes, "Do not forsake the assembly." God uses other believers to challenge and encourage us. Even the poet, John Donne, recognized the foolishness of isolation when he wrote, "No man is an island unto himself."

Through Christ, we can develop a mind that desires good. It's like the farmer who diligently looks after plants to protect them from weeds, insects, disease, lack of moisture, or overexposure to the sun. We can cultivate our minds through care, training, and study in order to encourage growth. Carefully nurturing one's mind to think critically takes effort but becomes more natural with practice.

Just as we are not to simply reflect others' values, we must not neglect a personal development of the mind. Critical thinking requires us to stretch ourselves, moving beyond the bubble of our mental comfort zone. Critical thinking also challenges us to reflect upon what we believe and value. As C.S. Lewis writes, "The right deference against false sentiments is to inculcate just sentiments. For famished nature will be avenged and a hard heart is no infallible protection against a soft head."[93] Unless we challenge ourselves to think critically, we will readily accept other opinions without thinking about the consequences of these ideas. In short, we are constantly in a process of transformation. This is especially true for Christians. Right now, we are *becoming* who we will be in the future. If we want to live productively using sound, reliable judgment, we must train our minds to think critically.

The only way you can keep your cool when the heat is on is to look for Jesus in the fire and walk with him.

– David O. Dykes[94]

CHAPTER

11

Between the
Lines

The need to think critically is always relevant, but never more so than today, in our Postmodern world. In 1947, author and speaker, Dorothy Sayers, addressed the issue to a crowd gathered at Oxford:

> *For we let our young men and women go out in a day when armor was never so necessary. By teaching them to read, we have left them at the mercy of the printed word. By the invention of the film and the radio, we have made certain that no aversion to reading shall secure them from the incessant battery of words, words, words. They do not know what the words mean; they do not know how to ward them off or blunt their edge or fling them back; they are a prey to words in their emotions instead of being masters of them in their intellects. We have lost the tools of learning, and in their absence can only make a botched and piecemeal job of it.*[95]

The "tools of learning" are all those qualities of critical thinking from the previous chapter: preparing, listening, thinking, asking questions, and making connections. It's being aware of what you're reading or viewing. It's being engaged in a conversation so that you really hear what the person in saying – not just thinking about your next response. For Christians, these "tools of learning" always start with Christ because He changes a mindset to one that thinks and acts like Him.

LIFE IN THE REAL WORLD

On the secular campus, one of the biggest challenges facing Christians is Postmodernism. At first glance, it's all-embracing, open-minded, and tolerant; it welcomes any other view in its search for truth. Within this view, all beliefs or values should carry equal weight, even if they are in stark contrast to one another. Somehow, we'll all just "get along" because we avoid confrontation or even simple discussion about the deeper, controversial issues in life. But the irony here is that those who take a stand for truth, specifically biblical truth, are labeled judgmental, intolerant, and narrow-minded. Postmodernism rejects absolutes. That means that even if you bring up specific verses to contradict false ideas, it's thrown out in the secular classroom because the Bible isn't taken as a final authority.

What that also means is that Christians really need to know *why* they believe what they believe. You need to know for yourself why the Bible is the ultimate authority. From there, Chuck Edwards of Summit Ministries writes, "You must do your homework twice. This means reading your assigned work and then researching a biblical view on the subject."[96] At times, presenting a biblical view in the classroom means doing extra research to support your faith with evidence. The following websites are excellent resources to make your research a little easier:

Organization	Area of Interest	Web Address
Summit Ministries	Christian Training	summit.org
Probe Ministries	Christian Training	probe.org
Creation Research Society	Creation	crsq.org
Answers in Genesis	Creation	answersingenesis.org
Christian Apologetics & Research Ministry	Research; Apologetics	carm.org
Christian Research Institute	Research; Apologetics	equip.org
Associates for Biblical Research	Biblical Archaeology	abr.christiananswers.net
Abort73	Abortion: Pro-Life	abort73.com

If Christians are to make an impact in this world, they must point others to the only source of absolute truth. This always starts with Scripture. The Bible provides real answers to all the questions of life and offers a personal relationship with God through Christ. Within its pages, there is freedom from sin, guilt, and even death. There is no reliance on man's limited ability to find personal meaning. Instead, as John 8:32 states, "You will know the truth and the truth will set you free."

That's how the glory of Christ is made evident on a secular campus. Real Christianity is different. It takes a stand based on the knowledge that God is who He says He is. There's real hope in a God who became man so that we could by saved from our sin and our selves. The truth of who Christ is and what He does in a life makes a person different. It's refreshing when feelings and opinions *appear* to be the final authority in our culture.

THINKING BETWEEN THE LINES

If we're going to share Christ on the campus, we need to communicate clearly and think critically. To do that, we need to recognize what we read and hear. That's called thinking *between the lines*. In their book, *Discovering Arguments*, Dean Memering and William Palmer point out that "one of the problems of reasoning lies in the fact that what is not said can be as significant as what is said."[97] Sometimes ideas carry assumptions and implications that point to a conclusion, but those ideas lack evidence. Thinking between the lines is just one approach to critical thinking. It involves looking for reasons and reliable sources behind ideas and indirect statements.

Take the idea of tolerance, for example. Tolerance assumes that if we all just agree to disagree and embrace others for who they really are, we'll be happy and get along. In theory, tolerance is peaceful. It's believed to be the keys to peace, love, and friendship. The reality, however, is that tolerance may not always embrace what is right. Real love is patient and gracious, but it also knows this: "Faithful are the wounds of a friend, but the kisses of an enemy are deceitful" (Proverbs 27:6). A real friend is honest, even when it hurts.

When something is assumed, it's accepted as truth – no questions asked. Keep in mind, however, that a statement can be true, even if a person doesn't directly explain the reasons behind the statement. However, we need to be careful if we *rely* on these statements as proof. To check out an idea, we need to look at what's beneath the surface. An assumption takes something in an idea or belief for granted. It takes the place of proof and depends on prior knowledge or experience. The problem with an assumption is that it's tucked into an idea to make the idea look and sound like truth. It leaves no room to explore other options.

Many people aren't in the practice of questioning assumptions, whether they are their own or those of others. To identify assumptions, you'll need to question the reasons behind an idea. What are the reasons beneath the surface? This is being aware of what is not said blatantly. Exploring these underlying reasons can expose false information and prevent problems. From there, it's important to ask questions.

1. What belief or action is being argued?
2. What reasoning or evidence is behind the idea?
3. Is anything taken for granted?
4. Are these ideas well-founded?
5. What does the Bible say on the issue? What specific verses support or reject an idea?
6. Could I accept the idea, even if an assumption is made?

Thinking this way brings discernment. It's the challenge of I Thessalonians 5:21: "Test all things; hold fast what is good." For the Christian, discernment is vital. This means we must be completely engaged in what's going on around us. If we are to "test all things," we need to examine issues by holding them up to the light of God's Word.

On campus, especially, it's important to pay attention to what's said, as well as what's implied. Author David Quine writes,

> *Let us highly resolve to discern the thoughts and ideas implicit in major statements made through art, music, literature, science, and government; so that (we) will be able to recognize what is not being said as well as what is spoken – in order to understand not simply what is written, but what is written between the lines.*"[98]

SUPPORTING YOUR BELIEFS

In Peter Kreeft's book, *Between Heaven and Hell*, the character of C.S. Lewis states, "The whole point of debating is not for me or you to win but for truth to win; not to see *who's* true, but to see *what's* true. I won't 'argue away' unless you're with me on this."[99] Lewis recognized that merely arguing with others is pointless. Few things in life are as obnoxious as two parties arguing just to hear themselves speak.

Knowing how to approach others when you disagree can be tough, but Proverbs 16:9 is encouraging: "The preparations of the heart belong to man, but the answer of the tongue is from the Lord." The Bible is the gauge of Truth by which all thoughts and actions are measured. Sticking to the biblical worldview gives a Christian the knowledge and discretion to choose words carefully. Of course, God ultimately does the work in a heart.

Before a Christian responds, it's crucial to study consistently and reflect on "the knowledge of the mystery of God... in whom are hidden all the treasures of wisdom and knowledge" (Colossians 2:2-3). Unfortunately, pride and zeal without knowledge does much to damage that which is credible. On the other hand, silence when Truth is required is just as damaging.

This makes a debate different from an argument. At college, you'll have opportunities to share you faith with others. Sometimes this will take place in an unexpected conversation; at other times, it will be more formal, like a debate. But the key to remember is this: *Truth does not need to be shouted in order to remain Truth.* Both sides of a debate have to use evidence in their arguments. To prepare you for this, I've adapted the following information from the wonderful resource, *Writer's INC*, "Becoming a Logical Thinker."[100]

- **Be informed.** Get accurate and reliable information from solid sources to support your views. You'll find that opinions are either strengthened or altered based on the evidence you collect.
- **Support your arguments with evidence.** Use facts, details, and examples to add reliability and strength.

- **Use conditional words like** *for example, sometimes, usually*, and *in most cases* to moderate your argument and add restrictions.
- **Stay focused.** It's tempting in a debate to wander off on side issues, but these issues should only be subpoints to the main argument being debated.
- **Make concessions.** By acknowledging weaknesses in your argument, you're actually showing balance and sound judgment.
- **Know when to quit.** As it says in II Timothy 2:16, don't keep talking when it gets into "profane and idle babblings." It's also time to stop when a debate turns into a circular argument.
- **Know when to come back.** Acknowledge when you are out of evidence to support your argument; you may need to return to the conversation after further research.

A CASE STUDY

Knowing what to say, how to say it, and when to say it can be challenging. While it's your responsibility to prepare for those challenges, God truly does guide and direct. Take Summer, for example. As a high school sophomore in Arizona, she faced the realities of living out her beliefs.

Summer was given an assignment to write a personal letter to President Bush on something that should be improved, supported by reasons. For her topic, she chose stem-cell research, the controversial issue of using cells to find cures for disease. The controversy of this topic lies in the origin of the cell, which can be extracted from adults or taken from discarded - but living - embryos. Summer's letter was thoughtful and well-supported. At one point, she included the testimony of a biochemist who stated, "The scientific literature overwhelmingly demonstrates that adult stem cells are already fulfilling the goals only hoped for with embryonic stem cells, making the destruction of human embryos unjustifiable." At another pivotal point in her letter, Summer wrote, "A human embryo is human; and it is still alive. Age is not what makes us human. Growth stage is not what constitutes a human being. Who are we to play God and decide who will die so that another may live?"

Standing before the class, Summer read her response aloud. At the end of her reading, her fellow classmates actually broke out in applause. The teacher, however, was not as impressed. In fact, she was so disgusted that she gave Summer a zero. The teacher also refused to send the letter in a packet to the president with the rest of the class letters.

The interesting part of this case lies in what happened next. How would Summer respond? At the teacher's request, did she change topics or rewrite her letter for partial credit? Would she compromise? Summer's following reflections on the experience reveal how her beliefs met reality:

I received no credit for my paper. I was confused, to put it mildly. I wore the façade that I was handling this with a straight back quite well. I confess that in 6th hour I slipped into a silent reverie, tears pricking at my eyes. What did I do wrong? Why was my letter worth zero?

After a few meetings with administration, I found out that my error was in expending too much effort. There was too much work and too much thought put into this assignment. This is not a sophomore level paper, and hence, it deserves no credit. I should rewrite this letter (for 75% credit) with only my opinion. I should strip it and leave it simply at "this is what I believe" minus "and this is why." Because obviously, dear teenager, you live in a time when you need not substantiate anything you believe, so please, take full advantage. With my 4.0 in jeopardy, I bounced one thought around in my head: how many ways can I say 'no'?

… Asking me to rewrite this letter, a letter that is so controversial in its very nature, whether or not I back up my statements, is asking me to change my entire worldview. It is never okay to have an opinion without reason, and I refuse to do so simply for a grade. If I am going to write so passionately on a subject, I certainly would hope that my word would not be so easily taken and swallowed just because I believe it is true. I am not so high as to believe that my word is truth based solely on the fact that I wish it to be true. I am a fallible creature. Would you not want me to give reasons for my beliefs?

… modern America thinks… it is no longer important to add reason to thought… whatever you want to be true is true.

As for me, I will not budge; perhaps I will take a beating for it. Well then, it is my honor. I would encourage anyone who may be put in my position to keep your chin level with the ground. The break in the bend comes from not having the courage to say 'here I stand, I can do no other.' A simple statement, yes, but a powerful one. It is my prayer that I do not speak only for myself when I say I prefer my grade to be in jeopardy over my faith.

We are the dangerous minds of America. We are the vulnerable, and we hold the future. I would absolutely love to be the most dangerous by challenging the core of backward thinking. I desire to contend for the faith, and always be ready to answer everyone who asks me about the hope I have.

Here is conviction that takes an uncompromising stand for truth. Yes, Summer was nervous about standing up to read her ideas in front of the class, and yes, it hurt that she was given a zero after so much thought and effort. With a 4.0 grade point average, Summer was risking a lot...

But was she really? Having convictions meant that Summer was *not free from fear*, but living by her convictions meant that she was *not trapped by fear*. Yes, Summer risked the potential mockery of her peers. Although that didn't happen, she did receive a lower grade and experienced the hostility of her teacher. The meetings with administration weren't easy either. But Summer was confident. She knew what she believed and why she believed it. She was wise because she knew God's truths and could defend her faith when it really mattered. This made her bold, even though she was young. As Summer proved, God hasn't given Christians a spirit of fear (II Timothy 1:7). What He has given us is a spirit of power, a spirit of love, and a sound mind. Like Summer, we can stand firm in our convictions, regardless of the consequences.

So now you're graduating. The prince of this world approaches. God keep you from fear, from faltering, and from faithlessness. Remember that the world is watching. What do they see?

– Elisabeth Elliot[101]

CHAPTER 12

Preparation for Life

SUCCESS IN THE DETAILS

College is just around the corner. It's not the ultimate end-all of life, but it does prepare one for living – regardless of whether that education is through a community vo-tech, a Christian college, or a secular university. As Dr. Ryken said, "Learning, in whatever form, is the student's calling. It is the arena within which you display good stewardship or lack of it."[102] God uses the circumstances in our lives to mold us and shape us into His plans for His glory. Wherever that may be, it definitely includes the next four years of your life.

Regardless of the college you attend or the career God has for your future, education is an opportunity for continued growth and, more importantly, to show others the glory of Christ. His glory is made evident through a Christian's life, a life of joy and peace in all things.

Unfortunately, however, some students don't show much joy or peace. They just plow through their studies without ever owning the experience. Their ultimate goal lies in a series of accomplishments, much like a to-do list for life: finish this semester, graduate from college, get a cushy job with great benefits, get married, buy a beautiful home, possibly have children, and enjoy the luxuries of this life – as if there is some point of "arrival." But really, is this true success?

In response to this question, I think Dr. Sproul said it best:

> *What is pleasing to God is not that much of a mystery: He has given us page after page of instructions as to what pleases Him. And so the ultimate goal of our lives is to be faithful in serving Him. There is much latitude in the many specific goals we can attain – in career, in family, in hobbies – while following the goals for a godly life as set forth in Scripture.*[103]

As Christians, we need to evaluate *why* we do what we do while weighing our actions on God's scale of success. While it's important to analyze ideas *inside* the classroom, it's also important to think about what goes on *outside* the classroom. This need for discernment reaches into the details of our daily lives. The question becomes, *what do we allow to influence us?*

Many contenders compete for our time and attention. Take, for instance, music, friends, and books, along with the media and our culture's buffet-style approach to entertainment. While these competitors can have a positive influence, they can also influence us for evil. How do those factors influence you? More importantly, what impact will you have on others? For the Christian, *what taste of Christ will you leave behind*?

Life is not put on pause, especially one's spiritual walk, upon college entrance. Some students are so thrilled by the idea of independence that they lose touch with all sense of reality. They forget – or maybe they never even realized - the purpose of their enrollment. Commitments and activities take over. Much worse, many Christian students don't make time to develop their relationship with Christ.

MAKING IT PERSONAL

If you end up on a secular campus, it'll be pretty obvious that your faith will be attacked from Day One. But a Christian doesn't just sit around and wait for the attacks to come. A Christian looks for opportunities to share the truth of Christ, to show the incredible difference that Christ makes in a life. That means you need to get ready *now*. If you're going to take a stand for biblical truth, you need to be able to support it with reasons. In a world where feelings and opinions appear to trump facts and reason, where do *you* stand on issues like sex before marriage, abortion, and homosexuality? What about tolerance, environmentalism, and animal rights? More importantly, what will you say when you're asked, "How do you know there's a God?" Or "Why should I believe the Bible?" Or "Isn't it narrow-minded to say Christ is the only way?" If your life is going to make any difference at all, it's not enough just to be moral or conservative.

For instance, take the following statistics from a *TIME* magazine report. Although these results relate to TV viewers, we can apply it to our college campuses.

> **According to a recent poll on television viewers, only 5% have ever complained to a broadcaster or the government, participated in a boycott, or demonstrated about indecent or explicit content on television.**[104]
>
> **Media commentator and television writer James Poniewozik adds, "Americans find TV too risqué, but that doesn't mean that they, personally, are offended. And while most want a stricter Federal Communications Commission (FCC), they don't back a ban on smutty content."**[105]

Through Christ, we can make a difference both on campus and in our community. We can speak out and write letters. We can use the minds God has given us to think carefully and communicate clearly. We can use our time, money, and talents to serve Christ and His kingdom. If we're going to make a difference for Christ in our culture, we need to be different. Who knows how God will use one voice to influence others?

Of course, real Christianity is so much more than just opposing cultural fads. It's not being afraid of what others think and value, a fear of offending the politically correct. Instead, real Christianity lives in godly fear – reverence – for what God thinks and values. Abby Nye, author of *Fish Out of Water*, writes, "Most of us have fears. But the difference between those who make a difference and those who sit silently on the sidelines, is not whether you feel the fear but what you do with the fear."[106] Real Christianity is completely sold out for Christ. It views the world as a place to be salt and light. The secular campus is a place with constant opportunities to represent Christ and His work that changes one's thoughts and desires. Real Christianity is not the open-minded, anything-goes tolerance of our culture; it's the Christ-like love that speaks the truth in all things.

At this point, you may be seriously considering going to a Christian college. However, my intent is simply to make you aware of what to expect. While opportunities for growth may be more obvious in a Christian environment, different types of situations still test your faith there. Don't be fooled into thinking that everyone who claims to be a Christian is one. It's easy to blend in on a Christian campus, to follow the rules without forming personal convictions based on God's Word. It's also easy to keep being spoon-fed the truth, instead of searching Scriptures for yourself.

No matter the school or job in your future, there are always opportunities to bring honor to Christ and make Him evident to others. These opportunities take place through your choices – mostly the little ones, the unexpected ones. At college, it's knowing when to speak out in class, when to meet with a professor privately, and when to say nothing at all. At home, whether reading a book for class or zoning in front of the TV, it's important to be aware of what we're absorbing:

> *If we already know what is good and right, part of maturity will be shown in self-censorship. Quality life always comes from making right choices, of choosing what we consider valuable. What do you want to put on 'the pages of your mind'? That's the question.*[107]

As students and workers, we need to evaluate what's "in" right now, what's "cool." If we fill our minds with trash, what do we expect?

Instead, we have a *choice* over the habits of our mind. If we really want to grow in Christ, we need to fill our minds with that which is true, noble, just, pure, lovely, and of good report, virtue, and praise (Philippians 4:8). We fill our minds by being grounded in God's Word through regular devotions and diligence in memorizing Scripture. It's amazing how God brings the right verse to mind at the exact moment it's needed.

Another vital part of a Christian's growth is meeting with other believers. That's why one of your most important priorities at college should be to join a solid church. The steadiness of a local church body will become like family. They may also offer a college group, a Bible study, or a mentor relationship to help you grow and keep you accountable.

On campus, many Christian groups meet for encouragement at college. Some of these groups include Campus Crusade for Christ, Navigators, and Inter-Varsity. These groups may create an outlet for witnessing and ministry both on campus and in the community. The beauty of joining such a group is that you realize you're not the only Christian on campus. In fact, you might even make some life-long friendships.

While outside groups are helpful, true growth in college and in life ultimately begins with Christ. Although life constantly changes, there's One who's always steady, always stable, always the same. For a Christian, everything in life revolves around this personal relationship with God through Christ. The desire for developing that relationship shouldn't change when a student enters college.

For Christian students who truly crave that closeness with Christ, college is, indeed, a place of preparation for life. It's not just a phase to get through, to see how much fun and entertainment we can cram into four years before "real living" begins. To come away from the college experience as a well-rounded, thoughtful, and growing Christian who views each moment as an opportunity to glorify God – *that* should be the real attitude toward the college experience. **Savor the time and thrive for life.**

Recommended Reading

An Annotated List of Additional Resources by Topic

WISDOM AND ADVICE

- To kick off this season of life, I highly recommend Elisabeth Elliot's book, *Taking Flight: Wisdom for Your Journey*. The book is divided into four major sections: following God's lead, encountering life's mysteries, seeking pure relationships, and making right choices. Divided into short chapters, each piece deals with such themes as trust, joy, and fulfillment. Elliot writes in an easy, straightforward manner based on her personal experiences. It's a quick read with practical advice for everyday living.

- R.C. Sproul's book Running the Race: *A Graduate's Guide to Life* is a compilation of selections taken from several of Sproul's other books but directed at the graduate. In his no-nonsense approach, Sproul answers common questions about faith, truth, the authority of the Bible, God's sovereignty, and the need for Christ. Although it's a short book, Running the Race is packed with wisdom and encouragement.

- John Piper's book, *Don't Waste Your Life*, is one of my all-time favorites. In it, Piper discusses what it really means to live for God's glory. It's not the job, but rather the way we live and act throughout each day that defines true success. Although the book is easy to read and understand, its biblical principles are challenging. It's also an excellent choice for anyone just beginning the career search.

THE CAREER SEARCH

- One source your librarian might recommend is the *Occupational Outlook Handbook*, published by JIST Works. Every other year, the U.S. Department of Labor updates this hefty compilation of more than 260 jobs. Job descriptions include training and education needed, skills required, wages, advancement opportunities, related jobs, and resources for additional information, including websites. JIST also offers an excellent resource with free career-related information at www.jist.com.

- *The Career Guide for Creative and Unconventional People* by Carol Eikleberry is an exceptional resource if you're unsure about which direction to take for a career. As the title suggests, this book helps those who don't quite fit today's mold. Eikleberry explains personality types in an easy, straightforward manner so that the reader can better find a field of interest. She also includes fresh tools for self-evaluation, real-life success stories, and a description of more than 240 creative jobs. I highly recommend this book because of its simple, practical information.

- *100 Best Careers for the 21st Century*, by Shelly Field, is packed with cutting-edge career ideas for today's job market. The book also includes details on the skills and experience you'd need to find a job in those fields. Careers are divided into topics such as healthcare, education, computer, advertising, communications, public relations, sales and services, home businesses, and more.

- *The Backdoor Guide to Short-Term Job Adventures* (4th edition), by Michael Landes, outlines a variety of short-term job or enrichment opportunities that may spark a future career. Different sections include outdoor adventure jobs, such as being a river guide or working at a ski resort; camp, ranch, and resort jobs; artist workshops; learning retreats; and volunteer ideas.

- In *Cool Careers for Dummies*, the authors provide more than 100 pages of "The Cool Careers Yellow Pages," a directory of interesting jobs based on your preferences for working with people, data, words, or things. Ideas range from becoming a locksmith to a home healthcare provider.

THE COLLEGE SEARCH

- ChristianityToday.com offers information on the college choice, financial aid, and life at college through its *Campus Life* magazine. Just click on the Christian College Guide to search Christian colleges by region. A profile of specific colleges includes religious affiliation, programs offered, extracurricular activities, and financial information. Viewers can also request catalogs or a call from the school's admissions office.

- A few years ago, some creative college students began an online service to profile individual colleges and universities. The *College Prowler* is now available both online and in books. Each book offers an in-depth study on one school with real quotes from actual students. In their efforts to be known as an unbiased resource, the *College Prowler* staff won't accept input from school officials (who've tried). A few of their 20 topics covered include academics, student housing, safety issues, and campus dining, among others. To see if the College Prowler has assessed your school (or for more information), visit <http://www.collegeprowler.com>.

- *Peterson's College Admissions Planner*, a packet for a three-ring binder, guides students and their parents through the admissions process. As an alternative to its bulky, 3,000-page book, *Peterson's Four-Year Colleges*, the *Planner* is a more practical and personal tool as students record observations and download applications or school profiles from the Peterson website at <http://www.petersons.com>.

○ A variety of other resources provides information on the college search, financial aid, and the transition from high school to college. For example, College-Bound, a branch from McMurray, offers services in admissions counseling and financial aid consulting. For online resources, check out <http://www.justcolleges.com> and <http://www.collegenet.com>. Of course, don't forget your library and local bookstore.

STUDY SKILLS AND TECHNIQUES

○ *Keys to College Studying: Becoming a Lifetime Learner* is, without a doubt, my favorite book on preparing for college. Co-authored by Carol Carter, Joyce Bishop, and Sarah Lyman Kravits, this book is stuffed with information on skills that build self-management, a positive work ethic, and leadership qualities. Unique in its approach to a range of preparatory skills, this book features relevant exercises to current issues, concept mapping as chapter summaries, and opportunities for personal application of study skills.

○ *The Great Big Book of How to Study* by Ron Fry is an excellent resource on reading and comprehension, memory development, time management, note-taking, library skills, computer skills, study skills, and test preparation. Look for other Fry books in the *How to Study* series, published by Career Press.

○ I've also enjoyed Brian Marshall's book, *The Secrets of Getting Better Grades: Study Smarter, Not Harder!* In it, Marshall includes hands-on exercises and activities with personal questions for self-assessment and goal-planning. Tips and techniques train the reader to earn better grades in any class. The Appendix includes a great list of web sites for getting better grades.

○ Eric Jensen wrote a wonderfully pointed and practical book, *B's and A's in 30 Days: Strategies for Better Grades in College*. Fun, entertaining, and illustrated, the book is organized as a day-by-day guide to grade improvement. Jenson's strategies include goal-setting, speed-reading techniques, study skills, and memory methods.

○ *Study Power: Study Skills to Improve Your Learning and Your Grades* is based on study skills used by students at Harvard University and Emory University. Its authors, William R. Luckie and Wood Smethurst, focus on time management to get the most out of every aspect of study. *Study Power* includes exercises and review questions.

- *Your College Experience is part of The Freshman Year Experience series.* Its authors, John N. Gardner and A. Jerome Jewler, cover a range of topics, such as time management, study skills, communication, career plans, use of technology, pressures at college, money management, and more. While the book is extremely helpful, some parental guidance is suggested.

CLASS DISCUSSION AND READING COMPREHENSION

- James W. Sire's book, *How to Read Slowly: Reading for Comprehension*, is a great introduction to exploring the bigger ideas in a piece of literature. Although the title sounds basic, this book is a wonderful resource for finding and evaluating an author's views. Sire's purpose is to equip readers to go beyond an initial idea to weigh an author's worldview from a Christian perspective. Included are key questions that help a reader sift and evaluate such views.

- English professor at Wheaton College, Dr. Leland Ryken is author of several books useful for literature and the classroom. Some of these include Realms of Gold: *The Classics in Christian Perspective; Windows to the World: Literature in Christian Perspective; and The Liberated Imagination: Thinking Christianly About the Arts.* I've also really enjoyed Ryken's edited book, *The Christian Imagination*, which includes excerpts from authors like C. S. Lewis, Francis Schaeffer, George MacDonald, and J. R. R. Tolkien.

- Although I've mentioned *Honey for a Teen's Heart* throughout this book, I want to highly recommend this great reference book. Co-authored by Gladys Hunt and Barbara Hampton, this excellent guide discusses how to use books as Christians. Their list of more than 400 books and annotations is sorted by genre or area of interest. Each annotation has been written in a manner that exposes any questionable material in order for the reader to decide which books are good, better, or best.

RESEARCH AND WRITING RESOURCES

- Without a doubt, the most straightforward book on writing is *Writer's INC: A Student Handbook for Writing and Learning* by Patrick Sebranek, Verne Meyer, and Dave Kemper. It's packed with everything you need to know about the process of writing and different forms of writing, including information about research papers and citing sources. I first discovered this gem while teaching at a public high school, but I've since used it in most of the classes I teach with homeschool students. If you choose not to buy the book, you can still check out the authors' website on MLA standards. Visit *The Write Source* at <http://www.thewritesource.com>. Look under the Research section to find the MLA style standards.

- A more formal book, sometimes required at the college level, is the *MLA Handbook for Writers of Research Papers*. If you decide to purchase a copy, bear in mind that these rules are updated continually as technology advances. Whether or not you purchase the MLA Handbook, check the most recent guidelines at <http://www.mla.org>. Click under MLA style to find a link for frequently asked questions.

- *Keys for Writers: A Brief Handbook* by Ann Raimes is an easy-to-use reference on rules of writing. Tabs make finding rules on grammar and mechanics easy. Examples are direct and to the point.

- *The Elements of Style* by William Strunk Jr. and E.B. White is a classic, concise book on basic rules of usage, composition, form, and style. Included are commonly misused words and expressions. According to the *St. Paul Pioneer Press*, "This excellent book, which should go off to college with every freshman, is recognized as the best book we have of its kind."

- *Research Strategies for a Digital Age* by Bonnie L. Tensen is the most helpful, current book I've found that combines traditional research with today's internet. Tensen, a computer instructor at a community college, provides excellent suggestions that will change the way you evaluate websites and incorporate their ideas into your papers.

PURITY AND RELATIONSHIPS

A Christian student's character at college reflects a view of who he or she is before Christ. This directly affects how a person approaches relationships with others. Although I have not devoted a specific chapter on the topic of dating, several excellent resources are available:

- John Piper's book, *What's the Difference?* is a quick read. In just over 80 pages, Piper defines the roles of men and women according to the Bible. It's a great response to our changing times as it explores the similarities and differences between genders, along with how these unique traits impact daily life.

- Elisabeth Elliot explores love and relationships in her book, *Passion and Purity*. In *Quest for Love*, she reveals true stories and answers real questions with her timeless advice and practical wisdom based on God's definition of love.

- In his book, *I Kissed Dating Goodbye*, Joshua Harris offers a unique approach to the world of dating. He calls a reader to re-examine the purpose of pursuing such a relationship in the first place, which should be marriage. My initial reaction upon receiving this book as a gift in high school was not exactly positive. However, the Lord changed my perspective on the issue as I kept an open mind. I now highly recommend this book for all singles, as well as the sequel, *Boy Meets Girl*, which explores a healthy relationship process.

WORLDVIEWS AND THE CHRISTIAN

- James W. Sire is one of the most concise and straightforward authors I've ever read on worldviews from a Christian perspective. Well-known for his book, *The Universe Next Door*, Sire provides readers with a basic introduction to common worldviews. In his book, *Chris Chrisman Goes to College*, Sire then explores the realities of life on a secular campus through the experiences of two Christian students. Practical and balanced, this book shows what it means to be an effective witness (without being obnoxious) in the face of contrasting belief systems. Other books by Sire include *Discipleship of the Mind* and *Why Should Anyone Believe Anything at All?*

- Summit Ministries is a Christian leadership-training center stationed in Manitou Springs, Colorado. Its goal is to equip today's teens with a defense for the Christian faith, so that they may stand strong with confidence at college and make a difference in the world. Currently, the ministry offers several conference opportunities, including eight two-week conferences during the summer, a one-week spring conference, and many Worldview Weekends, offered around the country during the school year. For more information, visit their website at <http://www.summit.org>. This site features curriculum, recommended reading, an online store, and a variety of other resources, including links to other organizations that offer information on worldview and apologetics.

- David Noebel, president of Summit Ministries, offers several excellent resources for understanding worldviews from a Christian perspective. His thorough resource, *Understanding the Times*, offers a revealing guide for understanding the ideas that have shaped our modern era. Noebel explores religious worldviews through ten different sections: theology, philosophy, ethics, biology, psychology, sociology, law, politics, economics, and history. This book has been revised into a course for high school seniors, which counts toward college credit in Philosophy, Bible, or Social Studies. With Tim LaHaye, Noebel has also co-authored the book, *Mind Siege*.

EQUIPPING THE CHRISTIAN MIND

- J. Budziszewski offers practical wisdom for a Christian at college in his book, *How to Stay Christian in College*. As a professor of government and philosophy at the University of Texas, the author has experience with today's college campus. He confronts commonly held myths and worldviews facing today's Christian students. With his no-nonsense approach, Budziszewski tackles tough issues using godly wisdom and insight. I highly recommend this book!

- In the book, *Love Your God with All Your Mind: The Role of Reason in the Life of the Soul*, J.P. Moreland connects the dots between a Christian's faith and the role of the mind. This book deals with the realities of developing a Christian mind, using logic in witnessing to others, worshipping the Lord with the mind, and working from a Christian worldview. This is truly an excellent resource for Christians seeking to strengthen and communicate their beliefs.

- *Fish Out of Water* is written by Abby Nye, a recent college graduate who confronts current issues on the secular college campus with a Christian worldview. Beginning with freshman orientation week, Nye deals openly with such topics as science and faith in the classroom, difficult professors and real life solutions, the many forms of liberal "indoctrination," and helpful campus groups.

- *Loving God with All Your Mind* is a fabulous book for young women who desire to take hold of their thoughts according to God's standards. Using her own struggles with fear, worry, and depression, the author, Elisabeth George, offers biblical truths for personal application. Topics include trust, perseverance, and contentment, among others.

- *Truth & Consequences* is a free monthly newsletter on worldview topics and other issues relevant for today's student. Available online by the staff of Summit Ministries, there are also suggestions to more excellent resources related to that month's current topic. Visit <http://www.summit.org>. Then click on Resources to find the *Truth and Consequences* newsletter.

- Lee Strobel, a former atheist, is a legally trained investigative reporter. In his book, *The Case for Christ*, Strobel investigates and reveals specific evidence that Jesus Christ is the Son of God. With its captivating interviews of various scholars, this book confirms the truths of the Bible. I highly recommend this book, which came at a crucial point in my life, when I was seventeen. It provided me with solid arguments at a time when I had many questions about the person of Jesus Christ. Other books by Strobel include *The Case for Faith* and *Inside the Mind of Unchurched Harry and Mary*.

- *Hard to Believe*, by John MacArthur, explores the costs of real faith in Jesus Christ, which goes beyond expectations of personal gain and prosperity. This book shows that true faith does cost us something, but the rewards of true fulfillment and eternal life are well worth any momentary costs.

- Check out the article "The Christian and the Arts" by James F. Williams. The article offers a balanced approach to appreciating art based on Scripture. Simply visit Probe Ministries at <http://www.probe.org> and type in the title to find this article, written May 27, 2005.

- *Books & Culture: A Christian Review is a bimonthly publication from Christianity Today.* This is a great resource on current issues in our culture from a Christian perspective, providing reviews on books, movies, music, and the arts. Interviews and personality profiles are also included. Specific topics cover science, philosophy, the arts, literature, and politics. Request a free sample or their weekly online newsletter at <http://www.BooksAndCulture.com>.

- *Character Out of Chaos*, written by David O. Dykes, is a brief but encouraging book on the development of Christian character in an age of moral chaos. This fabulous book shows how Daniel's challenges relate to today and how his choices affected his society.

Endnotes

Chapter 1

[1] Landes, Michael. Quote by Viktor Frankl. *The Backdoor Guide to Short-Term Job Adventures*. 4th ed. Berkeley, CA: Ten-Speed Press, 2005.

[2] Piper, John. *Don't Waste Your Life*. Wheaton, IL: Crossway Books, 2003. P. 32.

[3] Ibid., P. 76.

[4] Ibid., Ch. 8.

[5] Landes. P. 4.

[6] Nemko, Marty and Paul and Sarah Edwards. *Cool Careers for Dummies*. 2nd ed. New York: Wiley Publishing, Inc., 2001. P. 157-8.

[7] Moreland, J. P. *Love Your God with All Your Mind: The Role of Reason in the Life of the Soul*. Colorado Springs, CO: Navpress, 1997. P. 57.

[8] Piper. P. 140-1.

Chapter 2

[9] Leana, Frank. "Application Essays: Finding a Personal Voice." T*he Journal of College Admissions*: Fall, 1985.

[10] Stewart, Mark Alan and Cynthia C. Muchnick. *Best College Admissions Essays*. 2nd ed. Lawrenceville, NJ: Thomson/Peterson, 2002. P. 17.

[11] Hargadon, Fred A. "Advice from the Inside." *The Harvard Independent. 100 Successful College Application Essays*. 2nd ed. New York: Penguin, 2002. P. 7-10.

[12] Stewart and Muchnick. P. 23

Chapter 3

[13] Minnesota Higher Education Services Office. *Get Ready*. 2004 – 2005 ed. St. Paul, MN: MHESO. P. 22.

[14] Ibid., "Percentage of Financial Aid Awarded by Type." P. 22 Reprinted with permission.

[15] Marrian, Anna. "Struggling to Pay the Mortgage on My Mind." *Newsweek* 7 Feb. 2005, Vol. CXLV, No. 6: 18.

Chapter 4

[16] Huffman, Douglas S. New Student Orientation Devotions. 28 Aug. 2001.

[17] Allitt, Patrick. *I'm the Teacher, You're the Student: A Semester in the University Classroom*. Philadelphia, PA: U of PA P, 2005. Appendix.

[18] Fry, Ron. *The Great Big Book of How to Study*. Franklin Lakes, NJ: The Career Press, Inc., 1999. P. 161.

[19] Carter, Carol, Joyce Bishop, and Sarah Lyman Kravits. *Keys to College Studying: Becoming a Lifelong Learner*. Upper Saddle River, NJ: Prentice-Hall, Inc., 2002. P. 56.

[20] Morgan, Gary. Personal Correspondence. 8 Sept. 2005.

[21] Fry, P. 200.

[22] Carter, Bishop, and Lyman Kravits. P. 328.
[23] "Keys to College Success." <http://www.rong_chang.com/collsucc.html>. 09/22/04. Par 4.

Chapter 5

[24] Stevens, Richard and Thomas J. Musial. *Reading, Discussing, and Writing about the Great Book*s. Boston: Houghton Mifflin Co., 1970. P. 13.
[25] Sebranek, Patrick, et al. *School to Work*. Lexington, MA: D.C. Heath & Co., 1996. P. 485.
[26] Ryken, Leland. *Triumphs of the Imagination: Literature in Christian Perspective*. Downers Grove, IL: InterVarsity Press, 1979. P. 150.
[27] Williams, James F. "The Christian and the Arts." Probe Ministries. <http://www.probe.org>. 27 May 2005. Par 51.
[28] Chesterton, G.K. "Lewis Carroll." Originally published in T*he New York Times*. 24 Jan. 1932. *A Handful of Authors: Essays on Books and Writers*. Ed Dorothy Collins. Sheed and Ward, 1953. P. 112-19. *Nineteenth-Century Literary Criticism*, 2nd ed. Ed. Laurie Lanzen Harris. Detroit, MI: Gale Research Co., 1982. P. 113.

Chapter 6

[29] Sebranek, Patrick, et al. Quote by Donald W. McClosky. *Writers Inc: A Student Handbook for Writing and Learning*. Wilmington, MA: Houghton Mifflin, 2001. P. 275.
[30] Wyrick, Jean. *Steps to Writing Well with Additional Readings*. 6th ed. Boston: Thomson Wadsworth, 2005. P. 355.
[31] Booth, Wayne C., Gregory G. Colomb, and Joseph M. Williams. *The Craft of Research*. 2nd ed. Chicago: U of Chicago P, 2003. P. 15.
[32] Wyrick. P. 33.
[33] Booth. P. 14-15.
[34] Strunk, William Jr. and E.B. White. *The Elements of Style*. 4th ed. New York: Longman, 2000. P. 70.
[35] Tyler, Suzette. *Been There, Should've Done That: More Tips for Making the Most of College*. 2nd ed. Haslett, MI: Front Porch Press, 2001. P. 91.

Chapter 7

[36] Tensen, Bonnie L. "Preface." *Research Strategies for a Digital Age*. College Ed. Boston, MA: Wadsworth. 2004. P. Vii-Viii.
[37] Giddings, Thomas. "Colloquy: 'I would like to share...'" Online posting. 2 Aug. 1999. *The Chronicle of Higher Education*. 8 Mar. 2005. <http://chronicle.com/colloquy/99/webresearch/27.htm>.
[38] Rothenberg. David. "Use the Web to Connect with 'Ideas in Motion'." *The Chronicle of Higher Education*. 16 July 1999. 8 Mar. 2005. <http://chronicle.com/colloquy/99/webresearch.background.htm>.
[39] Booth, Wayne C., Gregory G. Colomb, and Joseph M. Williams. *The Craft of Research*. 2nd ed. Chicago, IL: U of Chicago P, 2003. P. 84.
[40] Rothenberg, David. "How the Web Destroys the Quality of Students' Research Papers." *The Chronicle of Higher Education*. 15 Aug. 1997. A44. *Media Literacy Review*. 8 March 2005. <http://interact.uoregon.edu/MediaLit/mlr/readings/articles/rothenberg.html>.

[41] Scott, Dr. Valerie B. "Colloquy: Searching the Web…" On-line posting. 2 Aug. 1999. *The Chronicle of Higher Education.* 8 Mar. 2005. <http://chronicle.com/colloquy/99/webresearch/28.htm>.

[42] This information was used with permission from Sandi McNamer, the Publications Director of the Wisconsin Department of Public Instruction; P.O. Box 7841; Madison, WI 53707-7841. Phone: (608)266-2188. Toll free, U.S. only: (800)243-8782. Fax: (608)267-9110. E-mail: sandimcnamer@dpi.state.wi.us.

[43] Tensen. P. 52.

[44] Ibid., P. 64.

[45] Memering, Dean and William Palmer. *Discovering Arguments: An Introduction to Critical Thinking and Writing with Readings.* Upper Saddle River, NJ: Prentice Hall, 2002. P. 526.

[46] Giddings.

[47] Rothenberg.

Chapter 8

[48] Ryken, Dr. Leland. "A Student's Calling" Address. Personal Correspondence. 8 Oct. 2004. The setting has been adapted, although this is Dr. Ryken's original address. Reprinted with permission.

[49] Dunn, Dr. David. Personal Correspondence. 3 Sept. 2005.

[50] Seevers, Dr. Boyd. Personal Correspondence. 12 Sept. 2005.

[51] Ryken. "A Student's Calling."

[52] Seevers.

[53] Grosz, Dr. Tanya. Personal Correspondence. 9 Sept. 2005.

[54] Allitt, Patrick. *I'm the Teacher, You're the Student: A Semester in the University Classroom.* Philadelphia, PA: U of PA P, 2005. P. 8.

[55] Sponsel, Dr. Leah. Personal Correspondence. 26 Aug. 2005.

[56] Billington, Dr. Clyde. Personal Correspondence. 29 Aug. 2005.

[57] Huffman.

[58] Billington.

[59] Ryken. Personal Correspondence. 25 June 2004.

[60] Ibid.

[61] Grosz, Dr. Tanya. Personal Correspondence. 9 Sept. 2005.

[62] Nelson, Dr. Randy. Personal Correspondence. 29 Aug. 2005.

Chapter 9

[63] Robinson, Ray. *Famous Last Words, Fond Farewells, Deathbed Diatribes, and Exclamations Upon Expiration.* New York: Workman Publishing, 2003, P. 38.

[64] Sire, James W. *Naming the Elephant: Worldview as a Concept.* Downers Grove, IL: InterVarsity Press, P. 122.

[65] Railsback, Dr. Gary Lyle. "An Exploratory Study of the Religiosity and Related Outcomes Among College Students." Doctoral Dissertation. University of California at Los Angeles, 1994. Summit Ministries. "The Importance of Worldview Training." Truth & Consequences Archive. <http://www. summit.org.> 2005.

[66] CIRP Freshman Survey, based on a 2001 survey of 281,064 students from 421 four-year colleges and universities. CIRP is the nation's oldest and most comprehensive assessment of student attitudes, and it is a joint project with UCLA's Higher Education Research Institute and the American Council of Education, based in Washington, D.C. Summit Ministries. "The Importance of Worldview Training." Truth & Consequences Archive. <http://www. summit.org.> 2005.

[67] Hunt, Gladys and Barbara Hampton. *Honey for a Teen's Heart*. Grand Rapids, MI: Zondervan, 2002. P. 80.

[68] Sire. P. 138.

[69] Sire. *The Universe Next Door*. 3rd ed. Downers Grove, IL: InterVarsity P, 1997. P. 48.

[70] Greive, Bradley Trevor. *The Meaning of Life*. Kansas City, MO: Andrew McNeel Pub., 2002. P. 6-7

[71] Robinson. P. 146.

[72] Ibid. P. 28.

[73] Sire. *Naming the Elephant*. P. 144.

[74] Sire. *The Universe Next Door*. P. 144.

[75] Lucas, George. *Star Wars*. Twentieth-Century Fox, Lucasfilm Ltd., 1977.

[76] Quine, David and Shirley Quine. *Let Us Highly Resolve: Families Living for Christ in the 21st Century*. Richardson, TX: Cornerstone Curriculum, 1996. P. 52.

[77] Sire. *The Universe Next Door*. P. 178.

[78] Although this is an attempt to clarify a theistic understanding of God, He is beyond man's complete comprehension. If we could fully define who God is, He would cease to be God.

[79] Le Claire, Paul. Sunday School Message. St. Paul, MN: Twin Cities Bible Church. January 30, 2005.

[80] Sire. *The Universe Next Door*. P. 200.

[81] Lewis, C.S. *Mere Christianity*. San Francisco, CA: HarperCollins, 1952. P. 63.

Chapter 10

[82] John Shipton works for High and Wild, an adventurous group that explores different areas around the world. For more information, visit <http://www.responsibletravel.com>. 2001.

[83] MacDonald, Gordon. *Ordering Your Private World*. Nashville, TN: Oliver Nelson, 1985. P. 96-97.

[84] Zaspel, Dr. James. "Debates and Logic." *The Connecting Link*: Vol. 3: No. 5, May, 2004. St. Paul, MN: Twin Cities Bible Church. P. 4.

[85] MacDonald. P. 97.

[86] MacArthur, John. *The Power of Integrity: Building a Life Without Compromise*. Wheaton, IL: Crossway Books, 1997. P. 43.

[87] Carter, Carol, Joyce Bishop, and Sarah Lyman Kravits. *Keys to College Studying: Becoming a Lifelong Learner*. Upper Saddle River, NJ: Prentice-Hall, Inc., 2002. P. 82.

[88] Budziszewski, J. *How to Stay Christian in College*. Colorado Springs, CO: TH1NK, 2004. P. 148.

[89] MacDonald. Ch. 9.

90. Ibid., P. 107.
91. MacArthur, John. *Successful Christian Parenting*. Nashville, TN: Word Pub., 1998. P. 80-82.
92. "Critical Thinking." Summit Ministries. Resources. Essays. <http://www.summit.org/resource/essay/show_printable_essay.php?essay_id=44>. 2004. P. 21.
93. Lewis, C. S. *The Abolition of Man*. New York: Macmillan Pub. Co., 1955. P. 24.

Chapter 11

94. Dykes, David O. *Character Out of Chaos*. Grand Rapids, MI: Kregel, 2004. P. 54.
95. Sayers, Dorothy. "Critical Thinking Fact Sheet." <http://www.summit.org>. 22 October 2005. Speech at Oxford, 1947. Quoted in "Trivium Pursuit," by Roy Maynard. (World, October 8, 1994, P. 13.) My emphasis added.
96. Edwards, Chuck. "Defending a Biblical View in School." *Truth and Consequences*. January 2005. Summit Ministries. <http://www.summit.org>. Par. 13.
97. Memering and Palmer. P. 333.
98. Quine, David and Shirley Quine. *Let Us Highly Resolve*. Richardson, TX: Cornerstone Curriculum, 1996. P. 63.
99. Kreeft, Peter. *Between Heaven and Hell: A Dialog Somewhere Beyond Death With John F. Kennedy, C.S. Lewis, and Aldous Huxley*. Downers Grove, IL: InterVarsity P, 1982. P. 34.
100. Sebranek. *Writer's INC*. P. 559.

Chapter 12

101. Elliot, Elisabeth. *Taking Flight: Wisdom For Your Journey*. Grand Rapids, MI: Baker Books, 1999. P. 111.
102. Ryken. "A Student's Calling" Address.
103. Sproul, R.C. *Running the Race: A Graduate's Guide to Life*. Grand Rapids, MI: Baker Books, 2003. P. 94. First printed in Now, *That's a Good Question!* P. 257-8.
104. "We Hate It! We Want It!" Poll: Watching Television. *TIME*. March 28, 2005. Vol. 165: No. 13. P. 29.
105. Poniewozik, James. "The Decency Police." *TIME*. March 28, 2005. Vol. 165: No. 13. P. 28.
106. Nye, Abby. *Fish Out of Water: Surviving and Thriving as a Christian on a Secular Campus*. Green Forest, AR: New Leaf Press, 2005. P. 187-8.
107. Hunt and Hampton. P. 63.

Index

100 Successful College Application Essays, 15

Allitt, Patrick, 29
American Psychological Association, APA, 54
Analysis, 44-45, 49, 78, 83
Assumptions, 76, 78, 95

Backdoor Guide to Short-Term Job Adventures, The, 3, 106
Best College Admissions Essay, 15
Between Heaven and Hell, 96
Billington, Clyde, 7, 72
Boolean system, 65
Brainstorm, 4, 56, 58
Budziszewski, J., 89, 110-111

Calendar, 22, 31
Campus tour, 11-14
Chicago style, 54
Chesterton, G. K., 45
"Christian Student's Calling", 67-69
Christian Theism, 82
Cliff Notes, 42
"College Comparison-shopping Chart", 13
Community college, 9-12, 109
Concept map, 37, 107
Connecting Link, The, 86
Cooperative Institutional Research Program, 77
Council of Biology Editors, CBE, 54
Critical thinking, definition, 88

Databases, 61, 63-64
Debate, 81, 96-97
Deism, 78
Discernment, 30, 78, 88-89, 95, 101
Discovering Arguments, 94
Don't Waste Your Life, 2, 105
Dunn, David, 69

Eastern Pantheism, 80
Edwards, Chuck, 94
Elements of Style, The, 94
Elliot, Elisabeth, 53, 100, 105, 109
Evaluation, 45, 49, 52, 88, 106
Existentialism, 79-81

Federal Communications Commission, 102
Federal Pell Grant Program, 25
Federal Trade Commission, 23
Fish Out of Water, 103, 111
Free Application for Federal Student Aid, FAFSA, 25
Fry, Ron, 30, 107

Gale Group, 21
George, Elizabeth, 111
Government service programs, 26
Grants, 11-12, 20, 25
Great Big Book of How to Study, The, 30, 34, 107
Grosz, Tanya, 71, 73

Hart, Lorenz, 75
Hillary, Sir Edmund, 85
Honey for a Teen's Heart, 78, 108
How to Stay Christian in College, 89, 110

Internal Revenue Service, 26
Interpretation, 51, 70, 81-82, 88
Interview, 4, 6-7, 15-16, 23, 53, 58, 111-112

Job-Shadow, 56

Keys for College Studying, 88
Kreeft, Peter, 96

Leana, Frank, 14
Lewis, C. S., 83, 91, 96, 108
Library of Congress, 64
Loans, 26-27
Love Your God with All Your Mind, 7, 111

MacArthur, John, 87, 90, 111
MacDonald, Gordan, 85, 87, 89, 108
Materials, 35
Marshall, Brian, 36, 107
Marx, Karl, 79
Memering, Dean, 94
Mnemonic Devices, 94
Modern Language Association, MLA, 7, 53-54, 108-109
Moreland, J.P., 7, 111
Motivation, 12, 24, 27, 30, 32, 48, 69, 73
"My Ideal Study Environment", 34

Naming the Elephant, 76
Naturalism, 79-80
Nelson, Randy, 74
New Age Movement, 80-81
Norgay, Tenzing, 85
Note taking, 40, 107
Nye, Abby, 103, 111

Odyssey, The, 44
Ordering Your Private World, 85
Outline, 39, 56, 58, 71, 106

PALBEG, 52, 62-63, 65
Palmer, William, 94
People-to-People International, 6
"Percentage of Financial Aid Awarded by Type", 20
"Personal Research Paper Checklist", 58
Piccard, Jacques, 85
Piper, John, 2, 3, 105, 109
Plagiarism, 52-53
Poniewozik, James, 102
Pope, Alexander, 79
Postmodernism, 79
Priorities, 30, 69, 104
Private college, 10-11
Probe Ministries, 94, 112
Procrastination, 32, 55

Quine, David and Shirley, 81, 96

Railsback, Gary, 77
Realms of Gold, 67, 108
Reciprocity, 11-12, 25, 27
Reflection, 44, 86, 88, 97
Respect, 40, 69-71, 74, 79
Responsible, 65, 71, 74, 79
Rothenberg, David, 61, 66
Ryken, Leland, 44, 67-70, 73, 101, 108

Sayers, Dorothy, 93
Schedule, 29-30, 32, 40, 57-58, 72
Scholarship, 12-13, 20-24
Search engine strategies, 61, 63, 64-65
Seevers, Boyd, 69-70
Self-discipline, 30, 71-72, 74
Shorthand, 32-33
Sire, James W., 76, 108, 110
Spark Notes, 42
Sponsel, Leanne, 71
Star Wars, 81
State university, 9-11
Stem-cell research, 97
Study-abroad, 36, 107
Study Smarter, Not Harder, 36, 107
Summary, 42-43, 48, 63
Summit Ministries, 90, 94, 110-111
Supporting evidence, 47-52, 56, 58
Syllabus, 29, 31, 71

Tax benefits, 26-27
Teachable, 2, 69-70, 74, 88-89
Test taking, 38-39
Thesis, 50-51, 58, 62
TIME magazine, 102
Triumphs of the Imagination, 44

Volunteer, 5-6, 24, 106

Walsh, Donald, 85
Westminster Catechism, 82
Williams, James F., 45, 112
Windows to the World, 67, 108
Works cited, 53-54
Work-study, 12, 20, 25, 27
Worldview, definition, 75-77
Writer's INC, 96-108

Zaspel, James, 86